Praise for the First Edition of *Raspberry Pi*

The Raspberry Pi is bringing back the golden days of experimenting with home computers, and Maik's book is an ideal starting point. The included projects are perfect for Raspberry Pi users of any age or level of experience.

➤ **Tony Williamitis, Senior Embedded Systems Engineer**

Schmidt takes a quick dip into many of the things you can do with a Raspberry Pi straight out of the box. I found it very useful for understanding exactly what I can use my Pi for, and it's given me some ideas for what I can do next!

➤ **Stephen Orr, Technical Enthusiast and Web Developer**

This is the owner's manual all Raspberry Pi buyers should get before they start diving in. It's clear, comprehensive, and succinct. I couldn't ask for more.

➤ **Thomas Lockney, Professional Geek**
DorkbotPDX

A wonderfully clear, concise, and useful introduction to the Raspberry Pi.

➤ **Michael Hunter**

Raspberry Pi: A Quick-Start Guide, 2nd Edition

Maik Schmidt

The Pragmatic Bookshelf

Dallas, Texas • Raleigh, North Carolina

Many of the designations used by manufacturers and sellers to distinguish their products are claimed as trademarks. Where those designations appear in this book, and The Pragmatic Programmers, LLC was aware of a trademark claim, the designations have been printed in initial capital letters or in all capitals. The Pragmatic Starter Kit, The Pragmatic Programmer, Pragmatic Programming, Pragmatic Bookshelf, PragProg and the linking *g* device are trademarks of The Pragmatic Programmers, LLC.

Every precaution was taken in the preparation of this book. However, the publisher assumes no responsibility for errors or omissions, or for damages that may result from the use of information (including program listings) contained herein.

Our Pragmatic courses, workshops, and other products can help you and your team create better software and have more fun. For more information, as well as the latest Pragmatic titles, please visit us at *http://pragprog.com*.

The team that produced this book includes:

Jacquelyn Carter (editor)
Potomac Indexing, LLC (indexer)
Cathleen Small (copyeditor)
David J Kelly (typesetter)
Janet Furlow (producer)
Ellie Callahan (support)

For international rights, please contact *rights@pragprog.com*.

Printed in the United States of America.
ISBN-13: 978-1-93778-580-2
Printed on acid-free paper.
Book version: P1.0—February 2014

Contents

Acknowledgments

Whenever I tell people that I'm an author, they look at me dreamily for a few seconds. Obviously, many people think that writing is about sitting at an old wooden desk, staring outside the window on a stormy day, and enjoying a good glass of red wine. For me this has rarely been the case, but still, most of the time I have a lot of fun while writing books.

I had a lot of fun writing this book, too—mainly because of the invaluable support of my editor, Jacquelyn Carter. She cheered me up on countless occasions, and her thoughtful advice made most of my problems disappear immediately. Thank you very much, Jackie!

As always, the whole team at the Pragmatic Bookshelf has been tremendously helpful and agile. Without you, this book would've been impossible!

This book deals with electronics, and I have created all the circuit diagrams with Fritzing.[1] I am deeply grateful that the Fritzing team has made such a great tool available for free. The Adafruit Fritzing library[2] has been tremendously helpful, too. Also, I have to thank Gordon Henderson for WiringPi.[3] It makes working with the Raspberry Pi's GPIO pins a piece of cake, and it saved me countless hours of debugging low-level code.

Simon Quernhorst kindly gave me permission to use screenshots of his great game, *A-VCS-tec Challenge*, in this book.

I cannot thank my reviewers enough: Daniel Bachfeld, Gordon Haggart, Michael Hunter, Thomas Lockney, Christian Müller, Angus Neil, Stephen Orr, Mike Riley, Sam Rose, Mike Williamitis, Tony Williamitis, and Jim Wilson. Your comments and suggestions made this book so much better.

Finally, I have to thank Tanja and Mika for being so patient and understanding. I am so glad I have you!

1. http://fritzing.org/
2. https://github.com/adafruit/Fritzing-Library/
3. https://projects.drogon.net/raspberry-pi/wiringpi/

Preface

Over the past decades, computers have gotten cheaper and cheaper, so today you can find them not only at your desk, but also in nearly every consumer electronics device, such as smartphones and DVD players. Still, computers aren't so cheap that you spontaneously buy one when shopping for your groceries. Usually, you carefully plan your next computer purchase, because you have to use it for a couple of years.

Computers like the Raspberry Pi will change the situation completely in the near future. The Raspberry Pi—or Pi, for short—is a full-blown desktop PC that costs only $35. You can connect it directly to the Internet, and it can display high-definition videos. Also, it runs Linux, so you don't have to pay for an operating system. This makes the Pi probably the first throwaway computer in history.

Originally, the Raspberry Foundation[1] built the Pi to teach children how to program, so it comes as no surprise that the Pi is an excellent device for exactly this purpose. On top of that, you can use the Pi for many other exciting things. For example, you can turn it into a multimedia center, use it as a cheap but powerful web server, or play some classic games.

The Pi is also a great machine for experimenting with electronics. In contrast to many popular microcontroller boards, such as the Arduino, the Pi runs a full-blown operating system, and you can choose from a wide range of programming languages to implement your projects.

With cheap and small devices like the Raspberry Pi, a new era of ubiquitous computing has begun, and you can be part of it. This book will help you get up to speed quickly.

---

1. http://www.raspberrypi.org/

Who Should Read This Book?

This book is for everyone who wants to get started with the Raspberry Pi. Even if you have some experience with other computers, you'll quickly see that the Pi is different in many regards, and this book will help you avoid the most common pitfalls.

You can choose from a variety of operating systems for the Pi, but this book's focus is on Debian Linux (Raspbian), because it's the most convenient choice for beginners. If you've never worked with Linux before, you should start with Appendix 1, *A Linux Primer*, on page 133. Even if you've worked with Linux before, you still might learn a few things, because running Linux on the Pi is different in some ways.

Of course, you'll get the most out of this book if you have a Raspberry Pi and follow all the book's examples closely.

What's in This Book?

The Raspberry Pi doesn't come with a user guide, but in this book you'll learn step by step how to get the most out of your mini-computer quickly. You'll learn how the Pi's hardware works, as well as how to run different operating systems and use the Pi for special purposes, such as turning it into a multimedia center.

Here's a list of all the things you're going to learn:

- The book starts with an introduction to the Raspberry Pi's hardware. You'll learn what the Pi's connectors are for and which additional hardware you need to start the Pi for the first time.

- After you've connected all the necessary devices to your Pi, you need an operating system. Although the Pi is a fairly young project, you can already choose from several operating systems, and you'll learn about their pros and cons.

- Installing an operating system on the Pi is quite different from installing an operating system on a regular PC. So, you'll learn how to get Debian Linux up and running on the Pi.

- Debian Linux runs fine out of the box on the Pi, but to get the most out of it, you have to tweak a few configuration parameters. For example, it's beneficial to set the correct layout for your keyboard. In addition, you'll learn how to install, update, and remove software.

- The Pi's hardware—especially its graphics hardware—is special in many regards. Depending on the display you're using, you have to adjust some low-level settings for the Pi's firmware. You'll learn what settings are available and how to solve the most common firmware problems.

- To see what you can achieve with the Pi with a minimum of effort, you'll turn it into a kiosk system. It will be able to display a set of static slides as well as live information from the Internet.

- At this point in the book, you'll have used the Pi more or less in isolation, but now you'll learn how to integrate it with networks. You'll use the Pi for everyday tasks such as browsing the Web, you'll make it accessible via Secure Shell, and you'll even turn it into a full-blown web server. Also, you'll learn how to share your Pi's desktop with a PC, and vice versa.

- With the XBMC project, you can turn your Raspberry Pi into a multimedia center with ease. Not only can you show your photo collections to your friends in your living room, but you can also play music in all popular formats, and you can watch your favorite movies and TV shows in high definition.

- The Raspberry team originally built the Pi for educational purposes, but you can easily use it to play some entertaining games. Even though it's possible to run some first-person shooters, you might prefer some classic genres, such as interactive fiction and point-and-click adventures.

- One of the greatest advantages the Pi has over regular PCs is its GPIO pins. In the book's final chapters, you'll learn how to use them to attach your own electronics projects to the Pi.

- The Pi's homogeneous hardware makes it easy to create additional hardware. The Raspberry team has released a camera, for example, that works perfectly with the Pi; you can easily integrate it with your own projects.

- The appendix contains a short introduction to Linux. If you've never worked with Linux before, you should read the appendix before you start with Chapter 3, *Configure Raspbian*, on page 23.

Where Can I Get a Raspberry Pi and Additional Hardware?

In the beginning, only two distributors in the UK produced and sold the Raspberry Pi: Farnell[2] and RS Components.[3] Today, you can buy a Pi from

---

2. http://www.farnell.com/
3. http://www.rs-online.com/

many other stores, such as Adafruit,[4] SparkFun,[5] and Maker Shed.[6] These shops also sell many accessories for the Pi, such as power supplies, keyboards, mice, and so on.

You can find a growing list of compatible hardware on the project's wiki,[7] but when in doubt, it's better to buy hardware from one of the vendors mentioned here.

Debian Linux

The most popular operating system for the Pi is Linux. Several Linux distributions are available for the Pi, and we chose Debian. In May 2013 the Debian team froze the latest version, named *wheezy*, and because of the great efforts of the Raspbian team,[8] it became quickly available for the Pi. Raspbian supersedes Debian squeeze, which was the reference operating system for the Pi for a long time.

The Raspbian distribution has many advantages over all of its predecessors. It is much faster, it has more recent software, and it is more stable. Also, it's the preferred solution of the Raspberry team, so this book's focus is on Raspbian.

Code Examples and Conventions

In this book you'll find a few code examples written in PHP, Python, HTML, and the programming language of the Bash shell. They're all very short, and if you've done some programming before, you'll have no problem understanding them. If you haven't developed software before, you'll still be able to copy the code to the Pi and make it run.

Online Resources

This book has its own web page at http://pragprog.com/titles/msraspi, where you can download the code for all examples, or you can click the filename above each code example to download the source file directly. On the web page, you can also participate in a discussion forum and meet other readers and me. If you find bugs, typos, or other annoyances, please let me and the world know about them on the book's errata page.

Now it's time to unbox your Raspberry Pi and have some real fun!

---

4. http://adafruit.com/
5. http://sparkfun.com/
6. http://makershed.com
7. http://elinux.org/RPi_VerifiedPeripherals
8. http://www.raspbian.org/

CHAPTER 1

Meet the Raspberry Pi

Before you start the Raspberry Pi for the first time, you should get familiar with its connectors and its capabilities. This will help you decide what kind of projects you can use the Pi for, and it will help you understand what kind of additional hardware you'll need. For example, you'll need a power supply, a keyboard, a mouse, and a display. In this chapter, you'll learn which devices work best.

Get to Know the Hardware

Unboxing a new Pi is exciting, but it certainly is not comparable to unboxing a new Apple product. Usually, the Pi comes in a plain cardboard box with one or two sheets of paper containing the usual safety hints for electronic devices and a quick-start guide.

The first version of the Pi looks attractive only to real geeks. It is a single-board computer without a case, and it's the size of a credit card. It somewhat resembles the innards of the many electronic devices you might have opened when you were a child. Later versions of the Pi might have a case, but until then we have to focus on its inner values, and that's what counts, isn't it?

What's on the Pi

The Pi is available in two flavors: Model A and Model B. Model B has been revised and is available in two slightly different versions now: Model B (Revision 1) and Model B (Revision 2). Model A is a bit cheaper and does not have as many connectors as Model B. I'll explain their differences and the differences between the two Model B revisions in detail in the following text.

I'll mostly cover Model B in the rest of this book, because it's much more popular than Model A. You can see it in Figure 1, *The front side of a Model B (Revision 1)*, on page 2.

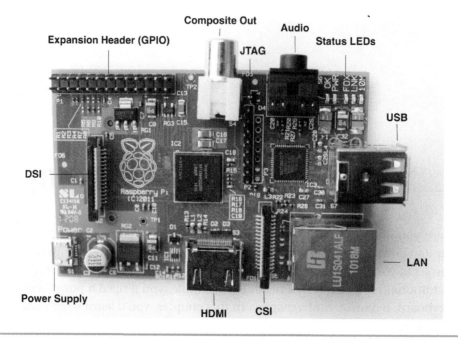

Figure 1—The front side of a Model B (Revision 1)

All Raspberry Pi models have the same heart and brain: a system on a chip (SoC) named BCM2835[1] that you can find in many mobile phones. It's cheap, it's powerful, and it does not consume a lot of power. These characteristics made it a perfect choice for the Raspberry team.

In contrast to a typical PC architecture, a SoC integrates a processor (CPU), a graphics processing unit (GPU), and some memory into a single unit. The BCM2835 contains an ARM1176JZF-S processor running at 700MHz, 512MB of RAM, and a GPU named VideoCore IV. First-generation devices and Model A boards have only 256MB of RAM. If you buy a new Pi, make sure it has 512MB of RAM.

For purists, the GPU is a bit problematic because its design and firmware are proprietary; that is, their source code is not publicly available. This probably will not affect you in your daily work with the Pi, but it is a problem for some strong proponents of free software. At least Broadcom has released the source code for the whole graphics stack under the BSD license.[2] By the time you read this, the Pi will probably be completely open source.

---

1. http://www.broadcom.com/products/BCM2835
2. See http://www.raspberrypi.org/archives/6299

The Pi has many connectors, and most of them look familiar. On a Model B board, you'll find two regular-sized USB ports that you can use to connect a keyboard and a mouse, for example. You'll also find a micro-USB port, but you'll need it to power the Pi, and you cannot use it to connect more devices. If you need to connect more devices, you have to connect them to a USB hub. The Model A board has only a single USB port, so you'll probably always need a USB hub.

You can connect the Model B to a network directly using its Ethernet (LAN) port. Model A does not have an Ethernet port, but you can add one by attaching a USB-to-Ethernet converter. Interestingly, Model B uses its internal USB hardware for networking, too, so there's no difference in networking performance between a Model B and a Model A with a USB-to-Ethernet adapter.

To connect the Pi to a display or a TV set, you have two options; the Pi has ports for connecting both HDMI and composite video. The digital HDMI standard is much more powerful than its much older brother, the analog composite standard. With HDMI, you can transmit high-definition video in crystal-clear quality, while the composite output is limited to what older geeks know as "the childhood TV." Using composite video, you cannot display high-definition graphics, and the output usually flickers a bit. Its biggest advantage is that many TV sets still have a composite connector, but HDMI is gaining ground quickly. By the way, the Raspberry team did not add a VGA connector, because it thinks that VGA is at the end of its life. Of course, you can use an adapter to connect the Pi's HDMI output to a DVI or VGA display.

With HDMI you can also transmit both video and sound, but if you're using composite video, you'll need a separate connector for sound output. That's what the audio jack is for—you can connect it to headphones, to speakers, or to your audio receiver using a standard 3.5mm plug.

To the left of the composite video connector, you'll see an expansion header that consists of two rows of pins. Most of these pins are general-purpose input/output pins (GPIOs), and you can use them to connect the Pi to other electronic devices. As you might have guessed from their name, they do not have a special purpose, so you can do many different things with them. For example, you can use them to connect your good old Atari VCS 2600 game controllers to the Pi so you can run your favorite 8-bit games in an emulator. In Chapter 9, *Tinker with the GPIO Pins*, on page 93, you'll learn how to use the expansion header, and you'll build a small hardware project.

On the board you can find several other connectors. The CSI connector[3] is meant for connecting a camera to the Pi (see Chapter 11, *Control the Pi Camera*, on page 121). With the DSI connector,[4] you can connect a display, and the JTAG headers[5] help you debug your hardware projects.

Every board has a few status LEDs. Model A boards have two LEDs, labeled ACT and PWR. Model B boards have five LEDs with slightly different labels depending on the board's revision. On Revision 1.0 boards, the LEDs are labeled OK, PWR, FDX, LINK, and 10M. On Revision 2.0 boards, their names are ACT, PWR, FDX, LNK, and 100. The LEDs have the following meanings:

- The *OK/ACT* LED indicates SD card access; it blinks whenever the Pi tries to access the SD card. You can control this LED by software, so it's not completely accurate.

- As soon as you connect a power supply to the Pi, the *PWR* LED turns on.

- The *FDX* LED shows whether your LAN is running full duplex.

- At every LAN activity, the *LINK/LNK* LED blinks.

- The *10M/100* LED indicates whether the Pi's Ethernet link is running at 10Mbit/s or 100Mbit/s. When this LED is on, the Pi runs at 100Mbit/s.

In the following figure, you can see the back side of a Pi, and you can also see a slot for an SD card on the right side.

Figure 2—The back side of a Model B

---

3.   http://en.wikipedia.org/wiki/Camera_interface

4.   http://en.wikipedia.org/wiki/Display_Serial_Interface

5.   http://en.wikipedia.org/wiki/Jtag

The Pi has no persistent internal memory, so you have to boot it from an SD card. You might have worked with SD cards before, because they are very popular as storage media in cameras, cell phones, and portable game consoles. They are available in different sizes and with different capacities, usually ranging from 1GB to 64GB (see the figure here).

Figure 3—SD cards come in various sizes.

What the Pi Does Not Have

Taking its cheap price into account, the Pi comes with a lot of nice things already, but it also lacks some useful features. For example, the Pi does not have a real-time clock (RTC) with a backup battery, and it does not have a Basic Input Output System (BIOS).[6] You can easily work around the missing clock using a network time server, and most operating systems do this automatically, but the lack of a BIOS is a bit more serious.

Simply put, a BIOS is a program stored in read-only memory (ROM) that runs on a PC at startup. Among other things, it's responsible for configuring new devices and for determining the boot order. For example, using the BIOS, you can specify whether you'd like to boot from your hard drive or from a DVD. The Pi has no BIOS, so it always boots from an SD card. Even if you have a perfectly valid installation of an operating system on a USB stick or an external hard drive, you cannot boot it. Of course, you can still use external storage devices, but you cannot use them to boot the Pi.

The Pi does not support Bluetooth or Wi-Fi out of the box, but you can add support for both of them using USB dongles. Unfortunately, most Linux distributions are still a bit picky about their hardware, so you should first check whether your flavor of Linux supports your particular device. (See *Where Can I Get a Raspberry Pi and Additional Hardware?*, on page xiii, for some advice about where to get compatible hardware.) All this is true for other types of hardware, such as microphones or webcams. As long as your operating system and your applications support your devices, you'll be fine. Otherwise, you'd better look for an alternative that is known to work on your operating system.

You now know what all the connectors on the Pi are for, and in the next section, you'll learn what devices you can actually connect to the Pi.

---

6. http://en.wikipedia.org/wiki/BIOS

What Else You Need

After unboxing the Pi for the first time, you'll quickly realize that the Raspberry team obeys the BYOP mantra—Bring Your Own Peripherals. The box contains nothing but the board; you'll need a couple of other things to get it up and running. You'll probably already have most of them at home.

Choose a Power Supply

First you need a power supply with a Micro USB connector, because currently the Pi does not ship with one. According to the Pi's specification, both models need a power supply that outputs 5V. The power supply should source 300mA for a Model A and 700mA for a Model B. Depending on the devices you connect to the Pi, it might have to source even more.

Many cell-phone chargers meet the Pi's requirements, and this is not a coincidence. The Raspberry team wanted the Pi to work with cell-phone chargers because of their ubiquity. I used the charger of a Samsung Galaxy S II for a couple of days, and it worked well for my first experiments. When I started to add more devices, it was no longer sufficient, and I replaced it with a wall charger from Belkin (see the figure here). It outputs 1A and works better, but for some hardware setups, you still need more power.

Figure 4—A USB wall charger

The Pi's biggest limitation regarding the power supply is that no external device should draw more than 100mA from any of its USB ports. So, as long as your keyboard and your mouse need 100mA each, everything works fine. Usually, you can find a small sticker with the power characteristics on the back of a device. If one device draws more than 100mA, sooner or later you'll observe strange effects.[7] To be on the safe side, use a power supply that delivers 1A to 1.2A for the Model B. For Model A it should be between 500mA and 700mA.

You can unburden the Pi with a powered USB hub, but it doesn't work with every product. So, before you buy something for your Pi, it's best to take a look at the project's wiki.[8]

---

7. http://elinux.org/RPi_Hardware#Power
8. http://elinux.org/RPi_VerifiedPeripherals

Choose an SD Card

Even with a perfect power supply, a Pi will not do much when you start it, because it needs an SD card with an operating system. You can buy preloaded SD cards,[9] but you can also start with an empty card and prepare it yourself. (See *Prepare a Bootable SD Card*, on page 17, for how to do this.) Usually this is the better approach, because it ensures that you get the latest and greatest software for your Pi.

Some users have reported problems with incompatible SD cards, so when in doubt, you should take a look at *Where Can I Get a Raspberry Pi and Additional Hardware?*, on page xiii. In theory, you can use a card of any size. Of course, the minimum size depends on your operating system, on the applications you're going to install, and on the data you're going to create on the Pi later. As often in life, bigger is better, and you should use a card with a capacity of at least 4GB for the most convenient Pi experience.

Connect a Keyboard and a Mouse

Unless you're planning to use the Pi as a headless system,[10] you'll need a keyboard and a mouse. You probably have a spare keyboard and mouse at home, and as long as they have a USB connector, they'll likely work with the Pi. Note that sometimes keyboards with an internal USB hub cause problems because they steal some current from the Pi that it might need for other things. If you experience strange effects, such as an unresponsive keyboard or infinite repetitions of keystrokes, try another keyboard or connect the keyboard to the Pi using a powered USB hub. It's best if your keyboard and mouse consume only 100mA each.

Some wireless keyboards and mice will not work properly because Linux does not support them all. In the beginning, be conservative and use wired equipment until everything works as expected. Then start to replace components one by one. If you run into problems, check to see whether your operating system supports your particular keyboard or mouse.

Often you'll need even more than two USB devices (or one, if you have a Model A), so you'll have to connect them to the Pi using a USB hub. Make sure the hub delivers enough current to power all connected devices. In nearly all cases, you'll need a hub that has its own power supply.

---

9. http://uk.farnell.com/raspberry-pi-accessories#operatingsystem or http://uk.rs-online.com/web/p/flash-memory/7631030/?
10. http://en.wikipedia.org/wiki/Headless_system

Choose a Display

Depending on the display you're going to use, you need an HDMI cable or a composite-video cable. If you're using HDMI and your display also has audio output, you're finished. Otherwise, you have to connect the Pi's audio jack to your sound system using a cable with a standard 3.5mm TRS connector. It's the same connector you'll find at the end of your iPod's headphones, and of course you can use those, too.

Choose the Right Network Equipment

If you want to connect a Model B to a network, you need only an Ethernet cable. The Model A does not have an Ethernet port, so to connect a Model A to a network, you need a USB-to-Ethernet converter or a Wi-Fi dongle.

Add a Case

Future releases of the Pi might come with a case, but until then you have to protect it yourself. Like every electronics device, the Pi is sensitive to dust and conductive surfaces, so sooner or later you should put your Pi in a case.

The Pi community is very creative, and people have already created cases using Legos[11] and even paper.[12] One of the biggest problems with most self-made cases is that they usually don't offer convenient access to the Pi's connectors. So, the best solution is often to buy a professional case—for example, from Adafruit[13] or ModMyPi.[14]

In addition to all the devices mentioned, you need a separate PC for some tasks, such as copying an image to an SD card or cross-compiling applications. So, all in all, setting up a Pi is not as cheap as it sounds at first.

A typical Pi setup looks quite messy on your desk after you've connected all cables (see the figure here). But despite its look, the hardware is ready for a first test run!

Figure 5—A wired Pi

---

11. http://www.raspberrypi.org/archives/1515
12. http://squareitround.co.uk/Resources/Punnet_net_Alpha3.pdf
13. https://www.adafruit.com/products/859
14. http://modmypi.com

Next Steps

In this chapter, you learned what all the connectors on the Pi are for, and you learned what additional devices you need and how to choose the right ones. In theory, you could start your Pi for the first time, but it won't do much without an operating system. In the next chapter, you'll learn what your options are and how to install a full-blown Linux system.

CHAPTER 2

Install an Operating System

Like every computer, the Raspberry Pi needs an operating system, and Linux is the preferred one for the Pi. That's partly because it's free, but mainly it's because Linux runs on the Pi's ARM processor while most other operating systems work only on Intel architecture. Still, not every Linux distribution will run on the Pi, because some don't support the Pi's particular type of ARM processor. For example, you can't install Ubuntu Linux on a Pi. In this chapter, you'll first learn what your operating system options are.

Choosing an operating system is only a first step; you also have to install it. The installation procedure on the Pi is quite different from what you're probably used to, but it's not difficult: you need to install the operating system on an SD card. In this chapter, we're going to install the latest Debian Linux distribution, but the process is the same for all operating systems. You can actually create several SD cards, each with a different operating system, so in the end you'll have a pretty versatile system that you can turn into completely different machines by simply replacing the card.

See What's Available

Linux is still the most popular choice for an operating system on the Pi, and it helps you to get the most out of your Pi. Also, many people are already familiar with Linux, whereas the other operating systems running on the Pi are a bit more exotic.

Even if a Linux distribution runs on the Pi, it will often look and behave differently from its regular desktop PC equivalent, because it might use a windows manager that doesn't need a lot of resources. Also, you won't find all of the applications you're used to, such as many popular web browsers or office products.

In addition, you'll face some limitations around installing the operating system. Modern operating systems are fairly big, and they ship on DVD or are available as ISO image downloads. These images and DVDs contain the full installation process for the operating system; they start a program that detects your computer's hardware, and then they copy all files needed to the hard drive. Unfortunately, you can't insert a DVD into the Pi and install it, because the Pi has no BIOS. (See *What the Pi Does Not Have*, on page 5.) You can't boot from an external USB drive, either. You also can't copy an ISO image of a DVD to an SD card. Instead, you need a snapshot of a system that has already been installed and that you can boot from.

So, you have to create or find an image of a Linux distribution that you can copy to an SD card, and it has to be compatible with the Pi. The easiest way to get such an image is to visit the download page of the Raspberry project.[1] At the time of this writing, you can find images for Raspbian (Debian wheezy), Arch Linux ARM, Pidora, and RISC OS. More operating systems will certainly appear in the future; at the least, Bodhi Linux[2] and openSUSE[3] are already available. Also, some clever folks are currently trying to port Google's Chrome OS.[4]

At the moment, the best choice for your first steps with the Pi is Raspbian (Debian wheezy). It fully supports the Pi's hardware, it comes with a full-blown desktop (see Figure 6, *The Raspbian (Debian wheezy) desktop*, on page 13), and it contains some useful applications, such as a web browser.

On top of that, it has a powerful package manager that makes it very easy to install more software. We'll use Debian in the rest of this book, and in the next section you'll learn how to install it. Note that we'll use the names Raspbian and Debian interchangeably.

The other distributions are very interesting, too, but they target a different audience. Still, I'll briefly describe them in the following sections.

Arch Linux ARM

Arch Linux[5] is very minimalist and assumes that you already have a fair amount of Linux knowledge. Arch Linux doesn't use many resources, and it has a nice package manager, so it's a good choice when you want to use the

---

1. http://www.raspberrypi.org/downloads
2. http://jeffhoogland.blogspot.co.uk/2012/06/bodhi-linux-arm-alpha-release-for.html
3. http://news.opensuse.org/2013/09/09/opensuse-arm-gets-new-raspberry-pi-images/
4. http://www.cnx-software.com/2012/04/19/building-chromium-os-for-raspberry-pi-armv6/
5. http://www.archlinux.org/

Figure 6—The Raspbian (Debian wheezy) desktop

Pi as a server. For a desktop system, Debian is more convenient, though, because by default Arch Linux doesn't ship with a desktop environment. You have to install and configure it yourself.

RISC OS

The Pi doesn't only run Linux; it also runs RISC OS,[6] for example. This comes as no surprise, because RISC OS was one of the first operating systems designed for the ARM architecture. It still has a lot of fans and is definitely worth a look. RISC OS is not free software, but it is available free of charge to Raspberry Pi users.

Coder

Coder[7] isn't really an operating system. In fact, it's just Raspbian, but with a special purpose. Some Google employees created it to offer an easy environment for people who are interested in learning about web development.

If you or your children are interested in developing web applications using HTML5, CSS3, and JavaScript, you should take a look at Coder.

In addition to regular distributions, special-purpose distributions are common in the Linux world. In Chapter 7, *Turn the Pi into a Multimedia Center*, on page

---

6. http://en.wikipedia.org/wiki/RISC_OS
7. http://googlecreativelab.github.io/coder/

75, you'll get to know Raspbmc, a Linux distribution that will turn your Pi into a multimedia center.

Even though you can't change the Pi's hardware easily, you can still turn it into many different machines within a second: simply insert an SD card containing another operating system.

If you don't know what operating system works best for you, you might want to try a few before settling down. Don't worry, because in the next section you'll learn how to play around with various operating systems using NOOBS.

Have a Look Around with NOOBS

The number of different operating systems available for the Pi can be a bit overwhelming for new users. Thanks to the New Out Of Box Software (NOOBS) project, it's easy to try out various operating systems.

NOOBS is an automatic installer for the Pi's most popular operating systems. At the time of this writing, it supports Arch Linux, OpenELEC, Pidora, RISC OS, Raspbmc, and Raspbian. Two different versions of NOOBS are available on the Raspberry Pi's download page.[8] You can download a fairly big zip archive (more than 1GB) that already contains all supported operating systems. Alternatively, you can download NOOBS Lite, which contains only the installer. It will download the operating systems as needed. To make sure you've downloaded NOOBS from a trustworthy server, check the zip file's SHA-1 checksum. (You can learn how to do this in *Prepare a Bootable SD Card*, on page 17.)

You need an SD card with a capacity of at least 4GB to install NOOBS. Before you install NOOBS, you have to format the SD card with the FAT file system. If you're not familiar with formatting SD cards on your operating system, take a look at the official tools for Windows[9] and Mac OS X.[10] On Linux, it's best to use gparted.[11]

After you've formatted the SD card, you can extract the zip archive and copy its content to the SD card. When you extract the zip archive, the content will be stored in a directory named NOOBS_v1_3 or something similar. Make sure you copy only the directory's content to the SD card, and not the directory itself.

---

8.   http://www.raspberrypi.org/downloads
9.   https://www.sdcard.org/downloads/formatter_4/eula_windows/
10. https://www.sdcard.org/downloads/formatter_4/eula_mac/
11. http://gparted.sourceforge.net/

That's all you have to do to install NOOBS. You can now put the SD card into your Pi and start it. NOOBS will greet you with a simple menu (see the following figure) showing all available operating systems. Use your mouse or your keyboard to choose as many as you like, and NOOBS will start a fully automated installation process. This installation process takes a couple of minutes.

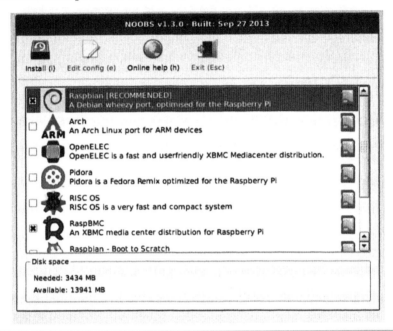

Figure 7—You can choose from a lot of operating systems in NOOBS.

In some rare cases, NOOBS will not detect the correct output mode for your display. Usually, you can fix this by pressing one of the following four number keys:

1. Sets the display mode to its default value—that is, HDMI.

2. Selects the HDMI safe mode. It may help when you've connected the Pi to a display using HDMI.

3. Try this option if you've connected your Pi to a display using composite PAL.

4. This option is for users who have connected the Pi to a composite NTSC display.

Also, NOOBS allows you to start a minimal web browser, so you can search the web for solutions to potential problems. If you've installed Raspbian using

NOOBS, you can also edit /boot/config.txt from the main menu. In Chapter 4, *Configure the Firmware*, on page 41, you'll learn what this file is for.

After NOOBS has finished the installation, boot the Pi, and it will allow you to boot one of the operating systems you've installed (see the following figure).

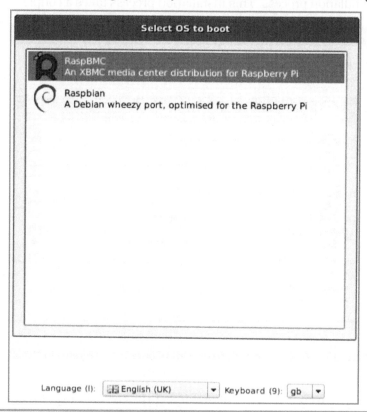

Figure 8—You can choose which operating system you'd like to boot.

If you'd like to remove an operating system or install another operating system, hold the Shift key while booting the Pi. This will open the NOOBS menu so you can choose another candidate. Note that currently NOOBS will always reinstall all operating systems, so you'll lose all of your data!

NOOBS is great for getting an overview of the Pi's best operating systems, but it has some disadvantages, too. For example, it doesn't support all operating systems available, it doesn't always contain the latest versions, and it needs some space on your SD card. So, it's often better to cleanly install your favorite operating systems directly on an SD card. In the next section, you'll learn how.

Prepare a Bootable SD Card

As you saw in Chapter 1, *Meet the Raspberry Pi*, on page 1, the Raspberry Pi doesn't have a BIOS or internal persistent storage. It has only an SD card slot. You use a separate computer to install the Pi's operating system on an SD card that you then use to boot the Pi. Fortunately, people have done this already for several operating systems, and they've kindly made available the content of such SD cards for free on the Internet. In this section, you'll learn how to transfer an SD card image to an SD card.

You'll need a PC with a card reader (which is quite a misnomer, because you can use it for writing, too) to modify the SD card. Some PCs have built-in readers, but you can also get USB readers for a few dollars. It doesn't matter which operating system you use, and we'll look at how to create the SD card on all major platforms. If you have access to a Windows box, I strongly suggest you use it, because it's easier and more convenient than Mac OS X or Linux for this particular purpose. Preparing an SD card on Mac OS X or Linux isn't rocket science, but you have to invoke a fairly dangerous command, and you can easily delete some important files. Also, on Windows you'll get more feedback while copying the card image.

No matter what operating system you plan to use for the installation process, you have to download the Debian image from the official download site.[12] You can download it using HTTP or via torrent. After the download has finished, you should have a file named 2014-01-07-wheezy-raspbian.zip on your local hard drive. (The filename might vary if a new version has been released.)

The procedures described in the following sections will be the same for images of all operating systems compatible with the Pi. You have to replace only the name of the image file.

Prepare an SD Card on Windows

Preparing the SD card on a Windows box is the most convenient alternative, because of Win32 Disk Imager.[13] This small application is free, has a nice user interface, and has a single purpose: writing images to SD cards. You don't even have to install it; you can just download the zip file from the project's website and unzip it to a directory of your choice. Double-click Win32DiskImager.exe, and you're ready to go.

---

12. http://www.raspberrypi.org/downloads
13. http://sourceforge.net/projects/win32diskimager/

Before you write the SD card image to an SD card, you can check whether the image is valid. So, you have to calculate the zip file's SHA-1 checksum. To do this, install the fciv command; Microsoft's support site has a lot of information about it.[14] After you've installed fciv, you can use it as follows:

```
C:\>fciv 2014-01-07-wheezy-raspbian.zip -sha1
//
// File Checksum Integrity Verifier version 2.05.
//
9d0afbf932ec22e3c29d793693f58b0406bcab86 2014-01-07-wheezy-raspbian.zip
```

If the long hexadecimal number is the same as on the download page, the zip file has not been compromised, and you can safely proceed. Otherwise, download the image from another location.

After the application has started, select the Debian image and your card reader's drive letter. Make sure you don't choose the wrong drive! If you do, you risk losing important data. Then click the Write button, and you should see something like the following image. Writing the image will take a few minutes, but then you'll have an SD card you can use to boot the Pi.

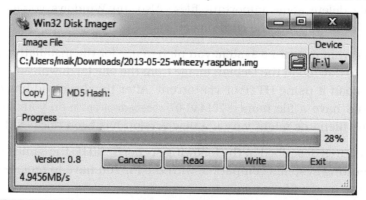

Figure 9—Win32 Disk Imager in action

Prepare an SD Card on Linux

Preparing an SD card for the Pi on a modern Linux system isn't too difficult, but you have to be very careful when performing the following steps, because you can easily destroy important data! Do *not* insert the SD card into your card reader right now. You'll do it later in the process to determine your reader's device name.

---

14. http://support.microsoft.com/kb/841290

Download the zip file containing the Debian image from the official download site, open a terminal, and change to the directory containing the zip file you've just downloaded. Although it's not necessary, it doesn't hurt to check the integrity of the file you've downloaded.

```
maik> shalsum 2014-01-07-wheezy-raspbian.zip
9d0afbf932ec22e3c29d793693f58b0406bcab86 2014-01-07-wheezy-raspbian.zip
```

If the long hexadecimal number is the same as on the download page, the zip file has not been compromised, and you can safely proceed. Otherwise, download the image from another location.

The following command unzips the image file to the current directory:

```
maik> unzip 2014-01-07-wheezy-raspbian.zip
Archive:  2014-01-07-wheezy-raspbian.zip
  inflating: 2014-01-07-wheezy-raspbian.img
```

Next you have to determine your card reader's location. Run the following command to get a list of all storage devices currently connected to your computer:

```
maik> df -h
Filesystem      Size  Used Avail Use% Mounted on
/dev/sda1        63G   15G   46G  24% /
udev            494M  4.0K  494M   1% /dev
tmpfs           201M  740K  200M   1% /run
none            5.0M     0  5.0M   0% /run/lock
none            501M  124K  501M   1% /run/shm
```

Insert the SD card into your reader and run the command again.

```
maik> df -h
Filesystem      Size  Used Avail Use% Mounted on
/dev/sda1        63G   15G   46G  24% /
udev            494M  4.0K  494M   1% /dev
tmpfs           201M  772K  200M   1% /run
none            5.0M     0  5.0M   0% /run/lock
none            501M  124K  501M   1% /run/shm
/dev/sdc2       1.6G  1.2G  298M  81% /media/18c27e44-ad29-4264-9506-c93bb7083f47
/dev/sdc1        75M   29M   47M  39% /media/95F5-0D7A
```

As you can see, on my system the SD card is named sdc, and it has two partitions named sdc1 and sdc2. Of course, this will vary on your system; that is, you might have more or fewer partitions, and your SD card might be named sdd, for example. Before you proceed, you need to unmount all partitions, so in this case you'll have to invoke the following commands:

```
maik> umount /dev/sdc1
maik> umount /dev/sdc2
```

As a final step, copy the image to the SD card. You have to run the following command with root privileges and make sure you're using the right device name for the of option.

```
maik> sudo dd bs=1M if=2014-01-07-wheezy-raspbian.img of=/dev/sdc
[sudo] password for maik:
2825+0 records in
2825+0 records out
2962227200 bytes (2.9 GB) copied, 460.427 s, 12.1 MB/s
```

Copying the image will take a few minutes, but if everything went fine, you'll have a bootable SD card that will bring Debian to your Pi!

Prepare an SD Card on Mac OS X

Preparing an SD card containing Raspbian on a Mac is very similar to preparing one on Linux, but there are a few important differences. You have to run only a few commands, but you have to be focused.

Do *not* insert an SD card into your card reader right now. You'll do it later to determine your reader's device name. Download the latest zip file containing the Raspbian image from the official download page. Open a terminal and change to the folder you've saved the zip file to. Then generate the file's fingerprint using the following command (this step is optional if you trust your download source or if you got the zip file from another trusted source):

```
maik> shasum 2014-01-07-wheezy-raspbian.zip
9d0afbf932ec22e3c29d793693f58b0406bcab86  2014-01-07-wheezy-raspbian.zip
```

If the hexadecimal number printed to the terminal isn't the same as the number on the download page, the zip file might have been compromised, and you should download it from another location. Otherwise, you can safely proceed. Unzip the file to the current directory.

```
maik> unzip 2014-01-07-wheezy-raspbian.zip
Archive:  2014-01-07-wheezy-raspbian.zip
  inflating: 2014-01-07-wheezy-raspbian.img
```

Now you need to identify your card reader's name. Run the following command to see all disk drives currently connected to your Mac:

```
maik> diskutil list
/dev/disk0
   #:                       TYPE NAME              SIZE       IDENTIFIER
   0:      GUID_partition_scheme                  *256.1 GB   disk0
   1:                        EFI                   209.7 MB   disk0s1
   2:          Apple_HFS Macintosh SSD             255.2 GB   disk0s2
   3:          Apple_Boot Recovery HD              650.0 MB   disk0s3
/dev/disk1
```

```
    #:                     TYPE NAME              SIZE        IDENTIFIER
    0:      GUID_partition_scheme              *500.1 GB      disk1
    1:                      EFI                 209.7 MB      disk1s1
    2:       Apple_HFS Macintosh HD             499.2 GB      disk1s2
    3:       Apple_Boot Recovery HD             650.0 MB      disk1s3
/dev/disk2
    #:                     TYPE NAME              SIZE        IDENTIFIER
    0:     FDisk_partition_scheme              *500.1 GB      disk2
    1:            Apple_HFS macback             500.1 GB      disk2s1
/dev/disk4
    #:                     TYPE NAME              SIZE        IDENTIFIER
    0:      GUID_partition_scheme               *1.5 TB       disk4
    1:                      EFI                 209.7 MB      disk4s1
    2:    Microsoft Basic Data MEDIA             1.5 TB       disk4s2
```

Your system's output will vary, but you need it only to identify your SD card reader. Insert the card into your card reader now, and after a few seconds, run the command again.

```
maik> diskutil list
/dev/disk0
    #:                     TYPE NAME              SIZE        IDENTIFIER
    0:      GUID_partition_scheme              *256.1 GB      disk0
    1:                      EFI                 209.7 MB      disk0s1
    2:      Apple_HFS Macintosh SSD            255.2 GB      disk0s2
    3:       Apple_Boot Recovery HD             650.0 MB      disk0s3
/dev/disk1
    #:                     TYPE NAME              SIZE        IDENTIFIER
    0:      GUID_partition_scheme              *500.1 GB      disk1
    1:                      EFI                 209.7 MB      disk1s1
    2:       Apple_HFS Macintosh HD             499.2 GB      disk1s2
    3:       Apple_Boot Recovery HD             650.0 MB      disk1s3
/dev/disk2
    #:                     TYPE NAME              SIZE        IDENTIFIER
    0:     FDisk_partition_scheme              *500.1 GB      disk2
    1:            Apple_HFS macback             500.1 GB      disk2s1
/dev/disk4
    #:                     TYPE NAME              SIZE        IDENTIFIER
    0:      GUID_partition_scheme               *1.5 TB       disk4
    1:                      EFI                 209.7 MB      disk4s1
    2:    Microsoft Basic Data MEDIA             1.5 TB       disk4s2
/dev/disk5
    #:                     TYPE NAME              SIZE        IDENTIFIER
    0:     FDisk_partition_scheme               *15.9 GB      disk5
    1:     Windows_FAT_16 RECOVERY              1.3 GB        disk5s1
    2:                    Linux                 33.6 MB       disk5s3
    3:      Windows_FAT_32 BOOT                 62.9 MB       disk5s5
    4:                    Linux                 14.5 GB       disk5s6
```

As you can see, on my Mac the SD card can be found at /dev/disk5. On your Mac, it might be at a different location. So, in the following command, replace /dev/disk5 with the location of your SD card:

```
maik> diskutil unmountDisk /dev/disk5
Unmount of all volumes on disk5 was successful
```

After you've unmounted the SD card, you can finally copy the Raspbian image to it. WARNING: the following command will copy the image to the device you specify with the of option. If you specify the wrong device—for example, your Mac's main hard drive or an external USB drive containing your most precious photos—all data will be lost. If you're absolutely sure that you've chosen the right target, run the following command:

```
maik> sudo dd bs=1m if=2014-01-07-wheezy-raspbian.img of=/dev/disk5
Password:
2825+0 records in
2825+0 records out
2962227200 bytes transferred in 496.170855 secs (5970176 bytes/sec)
```

The command will run silently, and it won't emit any progress messages. As you can see in the previous output, it took several minutes to copy the image to the card, so be patient.

When you create the SD card, watch out for one thing: some people have experienced read/write errors or unrecognized cards with SDHC cards on recent MacBooks and MacBook Pros with internal card readers. Using an external card reader should solve these problems.

Finally, you can eject the card.

```
maik> diskutil eject /dev/disk5
Disk /dev/disk5 ejected
```

That's it! You've created a bootable SD card containing Raspbian on your Mac.

Next Steps

Regardless of what operating system you've used, you should now have a bootable SD card containing Debian Linux. You also know how to transfer the image of every operating system that is compatible with the Pi to a bootable SD card. In the next chapter, you'll learn how to start Debian on the Pi for the first time.

CHAPTER 3

Configure Raspbian

No operating system or hardware will fit every user's needs out of the box. This is especially true for the version of Debian that runs on the Pi, because it comes as an image, which means you cannot choose all the configuration parameters that you usually enter at installation time. For example, the image comes with a fixed keyboard layout and locale. In this chapter, you'll boot the Pi for the first time and take a look around. You'll learn how to configure a lot of basics, such as your password and the time zone.

Boot the Pi for the First Time

Preparing the hardware and installing an operating system are important, but it's much more fun to actually boot the Raspberry Pi and see what it's capable of. So, insert the SD card you prepared in the previous chapter, and plug in the power supply.

If you've worked with Linux before, you'll recognize most of the messages pouring onto the screen. This comes as no surprise, because even if the Pi is an unusual computer, Raspbian still is an ordinary Linux distribution.

When you boot Raspbian for the first time, it starts a configuration program named Raspi-config. This program helps you configure the most important aspects of the Linux system. You can see its main menu in Figure 10, *Raspi-config makes most configuration tasks a breeze*, on page 24.

You're probably used to controlling user interfaces with your mouse, but you have to control Raspi-config with your keyboard. Use the down cursor key to move to the next menu item, and use the up cursor key to move to the preceding one. To select a menu item, press the Tab key or the right cursor key. This will highlight the Select button at the bottom. Press the spacebar or the Return key to select the menu item. Use the Esc key to leave Raspi-config.

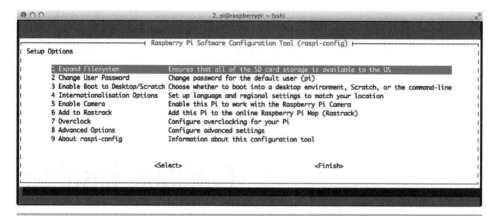

Figure 10—Raspi-config makes most configuration tasks a breeze.

To get familiar with Raspi-config, select the About raspi-config menu item. This will open a new window that briefly explains what Raspi-config is for. Click the OK button and press the spacebar to return to the main menu.

Most menus in Raspi-config also have a Cancel button. To cancel the current operation, press the Tab key until the Cancel button is highlighted, and then press the spacebar or the Return key.

The main menu has a Finish button that exits Raspi-config. Most changes you can perform with Raspi-config require you to reboot the Pi. So, when you press the Finish button in Raspi-config, it asks you whether you'd like to reboot.

Raspi-config will not start automatically the next time you boot the Pi. Don't worry. You can always invoke it in a terminal, like this:

```
pi@raspberry:~$ sudo raspi-config
```

In the next section, you'll learn what most of the Raspi-config options are for.

Customize Your Installation with Raspi-config

Before you do anything else with the Pi, you should adjust the most important aspects of your Raspbian installation with Raspi-config. For example, you should increase the space available on your SD card, and you should set the right locale.

In this section, you'll get to know the most important menu items in Raspi-config. You'll learn about the rest of the menu items later in the book.

Use All the Space on Your SD Card

The Raspbian image limits your root file system to 2GB. In other words, no matter what the real capacity of your SD card is, you'll be limited to 2GB. You could copy the image to a 16GB SD card, for example, but you still would only be able to use 2GB.

With the Expand Filesystem menu in Raspi-config, you can easily change this situation. Select the menu item, and after the next reboot, the Pi will grab all the space it can get on your SD card. Depending on your SD card's capacity and speed, this will take a while.

A few people have reported file system errors after they've resized the SD file system on an overclocked Pi. (See *Accelerate/Overclock the Pi*, on page 29, to learn more about overclocking.) In this case, rebooting the Pi usually helps.

Keep in mind that Raspi-config will not start automatically again. You have to log in with the username pi and the password raspberry. To start Raspi-config again, run the following command:

```
pi@raspberry:~$ sudo raspi-config
```

Change Your Password

At the time of this writing, you have to enter the username pi and the password raspberry to log into the Pi. If you're one of the lucky few who got one of the first boards, you also got a flyer with incorrect credentials. In previous releases the password was suse, so to be completely sure, check the credentials on the download page.[1]

Select the Change User Password menu item in Raspi-config to change the password. Raspi-config asks you for a new password, and it asks you to confirm that password. Note that for security reasons, you cannot choose simple passwords such as 123 or aaaa. If you want to learn more about users and passwords, take a look at *Manage Users*, on page 139.

By the way, raspberry is a really bad password—not only because it's easily guessed, but also because it contains the character *y*. For anyone without an English or American keyboard layout, this will lead to some frustrating login sessions. By default, Debian uses a QWERTY keyboard layout, but in Germany, for example, people usually use a QWERTZ layout. So if you're absolutely sure you've typed the password correctly for the tenth time, try raspberrz instead.

---

1. http://www.raspberrypi.org/downloads

Enable Boot to Desktop

By default, the Pi does not start a graphical desktop environment. Instead, it greets you with a plain terminal.

In *Start the Desktop*, on page 31, you'll learn how to start the desktop environment manually. The "Enable Boot to Desktop/Scratch" menu itemgives you the options of starting the Pi in command line mode, in desktop mode, or with the Scratch programming environment.[2] Scratch is a graphical programming language that makes it easy to create animations and games, even for children.

Remap Your Keyboard and Change Your Locale

By default, Debian assumes you're using an English keyboard layout, which might lead to some confusion if you're not. You can change the keyboard layout by choosing the Change Keyboard Layout menu item in Raspi-config's Internationalisation Options. This will spawn a configuration program that first asks for your type of keyboard (see the following figure).

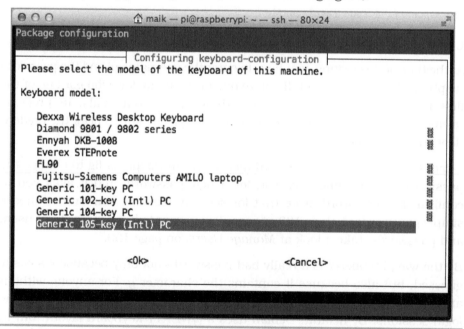

Figure 11—Choose your keyboard type.

---

2.   http://scratch.mit.edu/

Next, you'll specify the language you're using, and after that, you'll configure the behavior of a few special keys.

To enable the new keyboard layout, you have to exit Raspi-config using the Finish button and then reboot the Pi, but before that, you should consider changing the locale, too. A locale determines more than a mere keyboard layout. It determines how data such as text and dates get sorted and formatted, for example. Also, it affects the language the system uses to display information such as menu text in applications. In the following figure, you can see a German version of the LXDE desktop, for example.

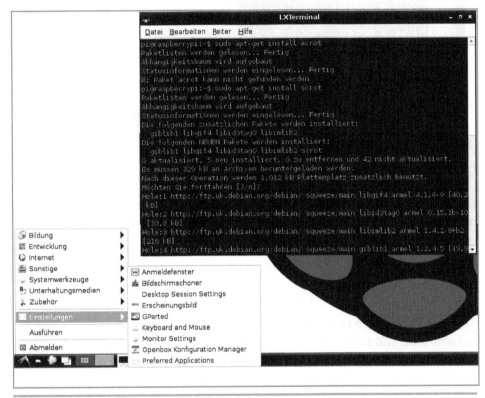

Figure 12—A German version of LXDE

You can configure your locale using Raspi-config's Change Locale menu. This starts a configuration program that greets you with the menu in Figure 13, *Generate your locale*, on page 28.

Here you can select which locales Raspbian should generate. You can select several and switch between them if necessary. Use the cursor keys to move through the list, and use the spacebar to select or deselect a locale. Using

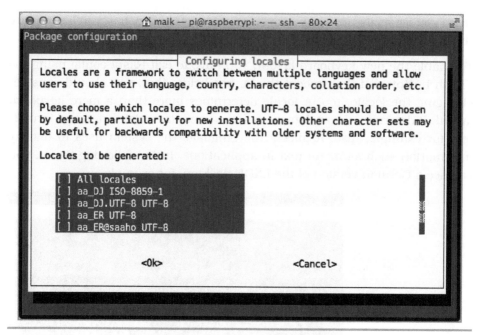

Figure 13—Generate your locale.

the Tab key, you can move the focus between the list of locales and the OK and Cancel buttons. Press the Return key to select a button.

After you select a list of locales and press the OK button, you can choose your default locale. Press the OK button again, and you're finished.

Set Your Time Zone, the Time, and the Date

To reduce costs, the Pi doesn't have a real-time clock, so it doesn't store the current date and time internally. Setting the correct date and time isn't just a nice feature; it's critical for cryptographic operations, such as validating certificates. You need correct time information for many purposes. Raspbian contacts a time server on the Internet when it boots and sets the current time and date automatically.

So, internally the Pi knows the exact date and time in the UTC time zone, but it doesn't know your time zone. That's what the Change Timezone menu item is for in Raspi-config's Internationalisation Options menu. Select it, and it will ask a few questions to determine exactly where you live. Then Raspi-config will store the time-zone information in your profile, so the next time you boot your Pi, the machine will know what time zone you live in.

If you haven't connected your Pi to the Internet, you can manually set the date and time like this:

```
pi@raspberry:~$ sudo date --set="2014-02-04 13:24:42"
```

This solution has a few disadvantages. It's not as accurate as it might be, and you have to repeat it whenever the Pi boots, so it's easy to forget it.

Enable the Pi Camera

The camera is a useful accessory for the Pi, and in Chapter 11, *Control the Pi Camera*, on page 121, you'll learn how to control it. Before you can use the camera, you have to enable it with the Enable Camera option.

Add Your Pi to Rastrack

Rastrack[3] is an online service that shows the locations of thousands of Pis on a map. If you want to make your Pi show up on the map as well, choose the Add to Rastrack menu option.

Accelerate/Overclock the Pi

By default, the Pi's internal clock rate is 700MHz. This is pretty fast for most tasks, but compared to the speed of modern PCs it's still rather modest. As with many PCs, you can overclock the Pi using Raspi-config's Overclock menu item. Here you can set the clock rate to 700MHz, 800MHz, 900MHz, 950MHz, or even 1GHz. This will increase your Pi's speed, but it will also lead to greater power consumption and a higher working temperature.

Note: depending on the quality of your power supply, overclocking can lead to stability problems or even damage the file system. In that case, hold the Shift key while booting the Pi. This will disable the overclocking, and you can then set a lower clock rate using Raspi-config.

Configure the Pi's Overscan Mode

The Raspberry team wanted the Pi to work with as many displays as possible, so they had to take into account overscan and underscan. In the case of underscan, the video output doesn't use the whole display size, so you can see a black frame around the actual video output. In the case of overscan, the opposite happens, so in some cases you can't see the whole output because it gets clipped at the display's borders. With the Overscan menu in Raspi-config's Advanced Options menu, you can enable or disable the overscan

---

3.   http://rastrack.co.uk/

mode completely. In *Configure the Video Output*, on page 43, you'll learn how to control video output in a more refined manner.

Adjust the Pi's Memory Layout

As you've learned, a Pi has either 256MB or 512MB of RAM. Let's assume you have the 256MB variant. Using the following command, you can check how much memory is on your Pi:

```
pi@raspberry:~$ free -m
              total        used        free      shared     buffers      cached
Mem:            186          37         149           0           5          19
-/+ buffers/cache:           12         174
Swap:           127           0         127
```

Oops! Apparently the Pi has much less than 256MB of RAM. How can that be? Don't worry: everything's OK with your hardware, and your Pi has 256MB of RAM. It just splits it between the CPU and the GPU (the device responsible for processing graphics). By default, the CPU gets 192MB of RAM, while the GPU gets 64MB. In most cases this is reasonable, but in some cases a different setup might make more sense. If you use the Pi as a server, for example, you won't need much graphics power, but you'll need more RAM for the CPU.

You can change the memory layout using the Memory Split menu item in Raspi-config's Advanced Options menu. Here you can determine how much memory the GPU gets. Choose the right amount for your usage and reboot the Pi.

Enable the SPI Kernel Module

The Pi is an excellent platform for creating electronic projects. In these projects you may use devices you can integrate using a protocol named SPI (Serial Peripheral Interface Bus). Such devices depend on a certain kernel module, and you can enable or disable this module using the SPI menu item in Raspi-config's Advanced Options menu. You'll learn a lot more about SPI in Chapter 10, *Working with Digital and Analog Sensors*, on page 107.

Choose the Audio Output

The Pi can output audio using two different channels: via HDMI or using its RCA jack. When connecting the Pi to a display using HDMI, it usually makes sense to output audio via HDMI, too. If you've connected the Pi to a display using its composite connector, you probably want to output audio with the analog RCA connector.

Under some circumstances the Pi cannot determine the correct settings automatically, so you have to adjust them manually. You can do this using the Audio menu item in Raspi-config's Advanced Options menu.

Start the Desktop

Unlike in other operating systems, a desktop environment is optional on Linux. So, it's not uncommon to have to start the environment manually. Alternatively, you can start a desktop environment automatically whenever the Pi boots. Choose Raspi-config's Enable Boot to Desktop/Scratch menu item to enable this behavior. If you rarely use the command line, this is a convenient option. Otherwise, the Pi will greet you with the login prompt:

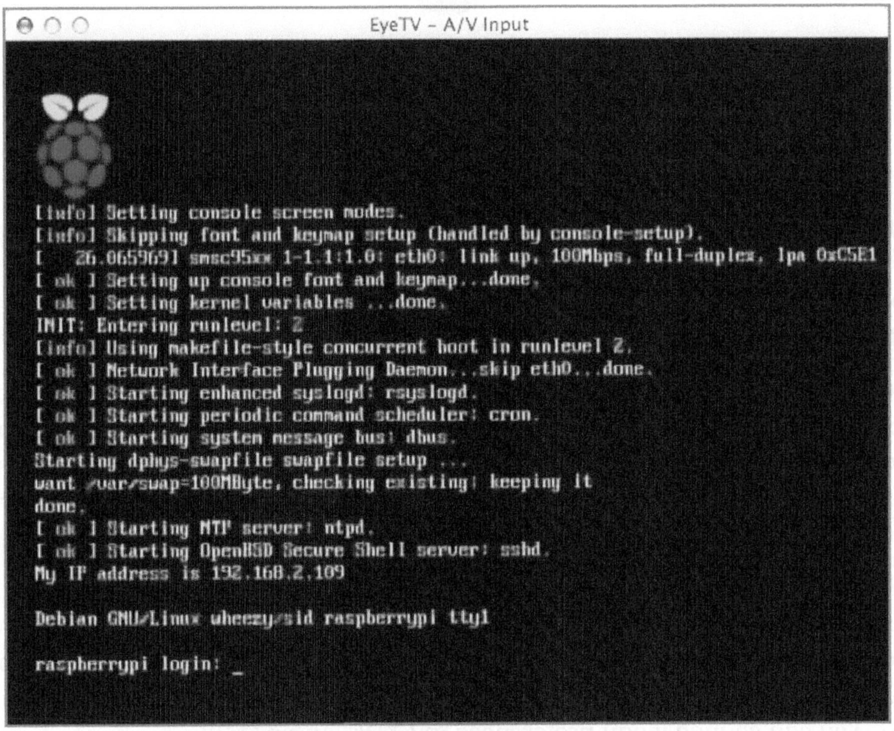

Figure 14—The Raspberry Pi's login prompt

After you've successfully logged in, you still won't see much more than a boring shell prompt. Use the following command to start the desktop and see some more colors. (It reminds you of the good ol' MS-DOS times when you had to run win to start the real action, doesn't it?)

```
pi@raspberry:~$ startx
```

After a few seconds, the Pi presents a nice desktop with a colorful raspberry in the background (see the following figure).

Figure 15—Raspberry Pi desktop

The desktop environment you've just started is named LXDE,[4] and although it doesn't use many resources, it still comes with some nice features. For example, it has virtual screens you can manage with the buttons in the toolbar at the bottom.

Starting applications is similar to starting them on Windows systems prior to Windows 8. Click the small LXDE logo on the left of the toolbar at the bottom of the screen to see which applications are available. Move the mouse to navigate through the pop-up menu, and start an application by clicking its name. In Figure 12, *A German version of LXDE*, on page 27, you can see the pop-up menu in action.

Also, you can configure a lot, such as the look and feel of all UI elements, the desktop resolution, and so on. You can change most of the settings using the system preferences menus; for example, you can see some of them in Figure 16, *You can change many preferences in LXDE*, on page 33.

To leave LXDE, use the small power-switch icon at the bottom right of the screen. If you've configured Raspi-config to always start the desktop, the Pi will shut down completely when you log out from LXDE. Otherwise, it will return to the boot terminal. To shut down the Pi from there, run the following:

```
pi@raspberry:~$ sudo halt
```

4. http://lxde.org/

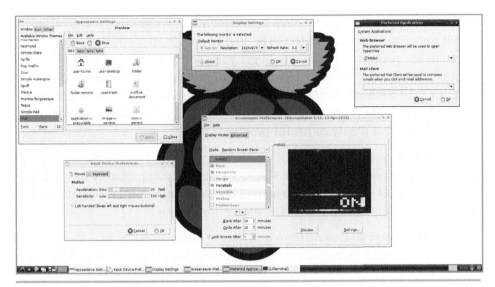

Figure 16—You can change many preferences in LXDE.

Manage Your Software with apt-get

Now that you have Debian set up, you probably want to add more software. Back in the old days, it was difficult to install new software on Linux systems. Usually you had to download a program's source code and compile and install it yourself. If the program depended on other projects or libraries, you learned about it when the compiler or the linker spat out some nasty error messages, and then you had to resolve the dependencies yourself—you had to download, compile, and install even more programs, and so on.

Fortunately, those days are long gone; all modern Linux distributions come with a package manager that automates the whole process of downloading and installing new software. Not only do package managers resolve all dependencies automatically, but they also save a lot of time by downloading binary packages instead of compiling them locally. Oh, and they help you get rid of stuff you no longer need.

Debian comes with a package manager, too; its name is *apt-get.* (apt stands for Advanced Packaging Tool.) In this section, you'll learn how to perform more operations, such as adding, updating, and removing software.

Install New Software

The Pi's Debian distribution comes with a minimal set of applications. This makes sense because the Pi doesn't have a hard drive, but to get the most out of the Pi, you'll probably have to install a few programs. The good news is that installing software on the Pi is no different from installing software on a regular PC running Debian. You'll get your software mostly from the same sources, and you can choose from many applications. Unfortunately, not all packages are available for the Pi's ARM architecture, and some applications simply don't run because they need more resources than the Pi has to offer. Still, you can find plenty of useful programs.

In this section, you'll install a PDF reader on your Pi. If you've worked exclusively with Microsoft Windows or Mac OS X before, you probably didn't worry much about PDF readers, but on some Linux systems—and especially on the little Pi—you can't take a good PDF reader for granted.

Interestingly, you can choose from a variety of different tools, and there's even a website dedicated to free PDF readers.[5] Two of these readers look especially interesting: Xpdf[6] and Evince.[7] You'll install them both, try them, and uninstall the one you don't like.

You can install new packages using the install command. To install Xpdf and Evince, run the following command (just make sure you're connected to the Internet):

```
pi@raspberry:~$ sudo apt-get install xpdf
pi@raspberry:~$ sudo apt-get install evince
```

Alternatively, you can install more than one package at a time like this:

```
pi@raspberry:~$ sudo apt-get install xpdf evince
```

Note that the most recent version of Raspbian installs Xpdf by default. In that case, apt-get will tell you that Xpdf is installed already.

Now you have both PDF readers installed as independent packages, and you can start and test them to see which one better suits your needs. You can find shortcuts for both applications in the Graphics section of the LXDE desktop's start menu. Also, you can start them from a terminal by running either of the following (only if you've started the desktop environment before):

```
pi@raspberry:~$ evince
```

or:

```
pi@raspberry:~$ xpdf
```

---

5. http://pdfreaders.org/
6. http://www.foolabs.com/xpdf/
7. http://projects.gnome.org/evince/

In the following figure, you can see both programs in action rendering the same PDF document.

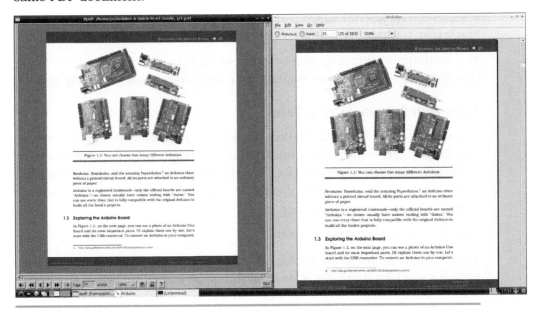

Figure 17—Two PDF readers showing the same document

Remove Software

Play around with both applications for a while and see which one you like best. Let's assume that you prefer Evince; you can uninstall Xpdf using the following command:

```
pi@raspberry:~$ sudo apt-get purge xpdf
Reading package lists... Done
Building dependency tree
Reading state information... Done
The following packages were automatically installed and are no
longer required:
  cups-bsd cups-client fonts-droid ghostscript lesstif2
  libcupsimage2 libfile-copy-recursive-perl libgs9 libgs9-common
  libijs-0.35 libpaper-utils libpaper1 libpoppler19 libxp6 poppler-data
  poppler-utils update-inetd
Use 'apt-get autoremove' to remove them.
The following packages will be REMOVED:
  xpdf*
0 upgraded, 0 newly installed, 1 to remove and 24 not upgraded.
After this operation, 404 kB disk space will be freed.
Do you want to continue [Y/n]?
(Reading database ... 60245 files and directories currently installed.)
Removing xpdf ...
```

```
Purging configuration files for xpdf ...
Processing triggers for mime-support ...
Processing triggers for man-db ...
Processing triggers for menu ...
Processing triggers for desktop-file-utils ...
```

The Xpdf application is gone now, without any trace. If you want to remove the application but keep its configuration files, use remove instead of purge.

Keep Your Software Up to Date

To make the software installation process as easy and as unobtrusive as possible, apt-get comes with a small database containing a list of all available packages and their dependencies. This database consists of only a few files. You usually won't work with it directly, but you should run the following command occasionally to update it:

```
pi@raspberry:~$ sudo apt-get update
```

This downloads the latest package lists from a central server and updates apt-get's local database. So, if you run the apt-get command before you install a new package, you can be sure that you will get the latest version available. Note that in some cases you have to run this command twice. apt-get is nice enough to tell you when this is the case.

If you've already installed software on your Pi using apt-get, you'll probably want to update it from time to time. The following command upgrades all software that is currently installed on your Pi:

```
pi@raspberry:~$ sudo apt-get upgrade
```

Running this command will take a while, but when it's finished you'll have the latest version of every single application and library on your Pi. For this, apt-get has to download a lot of files that you no longer need after apt-get has installed the applications. You can delete these obsolete files easily.

```
pi@raspberry:~$ sudo apt-get autoclean
Reading package lists... Done
Building dependency tree...
Reading state information... Done
```

Sometimes dependencies between packages and package versions change, so you might not need some of the installed packages anymore. You can remove them using the following command:

```
pi@raspberry:~$ sudo apt-get autoremove
Reading package lists... Done
Building dependency tree
Reading state information... Done
```

```
The following packages will be REMOVED:
ghostscript lesstif2 libxp6 poppler-data poppler-utils
0 upgraded, 0 newly installed, 5 to remove and 0 not upgraded.
After this operation, 15.3 MB disk space will be freed.
Do you want to continue [Y/n]?
(Reading database ... 49185 files and directories currently installed.)
Removing ghostscript ...
Removing lesstif2 ...
Removing libxp6 ...
Removing poppler-data ...
Removing poppler-utils ...
Processing triggers for man-db ...
```

In theory, this is all you need to know about managing software on a Debian system. There is one more helpful tool that you should know about, which you'll learn about in the next section.

Find Packages with apt-file

If you know the exact name of a package you'd like to install, apt-get is all you need, but in some cases you might not know the name. For example, you still have to install a lot of software from source and compile it yourself. If this software depends on a certain library that you don't have installed, the compiler or the linker will stop with an error message. Usually, the error message contains the missing file's name, so it would be great to have a tool that searches for all packages that contain this file. apt-file is such a tool, and you can install it as follows:

pi@raspberry:~$ **sudo apt-get install apt-file**

Like apt-get, the apt-file command depends on a local database containing a list of all packages and their dependencies. To update this database, you should run the following command:

pi@raspberry:~$ **sudo apt-file update**

Now you can use apt-file to search for a package containing a certain file. Let's assume you've heard about a cool PDF reader for the Pi named Evince, and you don't know which package you have to install to use it. The command shown here is all you need:

pi@raspberry:~$ **apt-file -l search evince**
```
evince
evince-common
evince-dbg
evince-gtk
gir1.0-evince-2.30
libevince-dev
libevince2
python-evince
```

This outputs a list of all packages referring to Evince so you can decide which one you'd like to install.

You can also use apt-file to list the contents of a package, even if you haven't installed the package.

```
pi@raspberry:~$ apt-file list evince
```

Package managers are really helpful, and every modern Linux distribution has one. On Debian it's apt-get, on Fedora it's yum, and on Arch Linux it's pacman. Although they differ slightly in their syntax, they all offer the same operations and behavior.

Install Software and Media Using the Pi Store

At the end of 2012, the Raspberry Pi Foundation launched the Pi Store[8] together with IndieCity[9] and Velocix.[10] In the store, you can find free and commercial applications, games, development tools, and media such as magazines or videos. The store offers two types of commercial applications: you have to pay a fee upfront for some, while for others you can make a donation if you like the application.

The Pi Store is available as a website, but it's much more convenient to use its native client (see Figure 18, *The Pi Store has a native client*, on page 39). The latest Raspbian image contains the Pi Store client, and you can launch it by double-clicking its icon on the desktop.

If you don't already have the Pi Store client, you can install it using the following commands:

```
pi@raspberry:~$ sudo apt-get update
pi@raspberry:~$ sudo apt-get install pistore
```

The application is fairly self-explanatory. After you've logged in, you can install software with a single mouse click. At the moment, the store contains only a few items, but taking the Pi's popularity into account, that might change soon. One title is particularly interesting: *Iridium Rising*[11] is an exclusive game for the Pi. It's free, and it looks very professional.

---

8.   http://store.raspberrypi.com/
9.   http://www.indiecity.com/
10. http://www.velocix.com/
11. http://store.raspberrypi.com/projects/iridiumrising

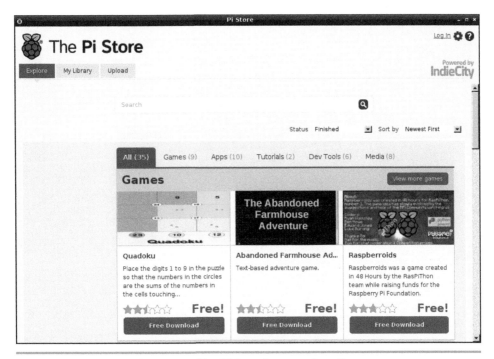

Figure 18—The Pi Store has a native client.

Next Steps

In this chapter, you booted the Pi for the first time, and you configured many aspects to suit your personal preferences. Also, you learned how to manage software on the Pi—how to install, update, and remove it.

Installing and configuring the Pi's operating system are important steps, but in contrast to regular PCs, the Pi needs some more configuration. In the next chapter, you'll learn about the Pi's firmware and how to adjust it to your needs.

CHAPTER 4

Configure the Firmware

The Pi needs not only an operating system, but also firmware that controls its hardware on a low level. For example, the firmware controls and configures the GPU, the card reader, and in some regards even the CPU. It's a vital piece of the Raspberry Pi, and you can solve many issues, such as problems with the video output, by setting the correct parameters. In this chapter, you'll learn how to configure and update the Pi's firmware.

Also, you have to update the Linux kernel itself from time to time. The kernel is the heart of a Linux system, because it manages all processes and the hardware. All applications depend on the kernel, and in this chapter, you'll learn how to keep it up to date.

Update the Firmware and Kernel

The Debian image already comes with firmware for the Pi, but the developers of the Linux kernel and the Pi's firmware release updates frequently. New releases usually contain bug fixes and improvements, so it's beneficial to update both the kernel and the firmware from time to time. To check which versions of the kernel and firmware are installed on your Pi, run the following commands:

```
pi@raspberrypi ~ $ uname -a
Linux raspberrypi 3.10.25+ #622 PREEMPT Fri Jan 3 18:41:00 GMT 2014 armv6l GNU/Linux
pi@raspberrypi ~ $ /opt/vc/bin/vcgencmd version
Jan  6 2014 21:16:43
Copyright (c) 2012 Broadcom
version b00bb3ae73bd2799df0e938b7a5f17f45303fb53 (clean) (release)
```

You can find the latest version of all files on GitHub,[1] and you can download them to the SD card. To install a new kernel and new firmware, you have to

---

1. https://github.com/raspberrypi/firmware

replace a few files in the Pi's /boot directory. The /boot directory belongs to the SD card's boot partition, which is formatted with the FAT file system. So, you can read and write it not only with the Pi, but also with nearly every computer in the world. In the following screen capture, you can see its content:

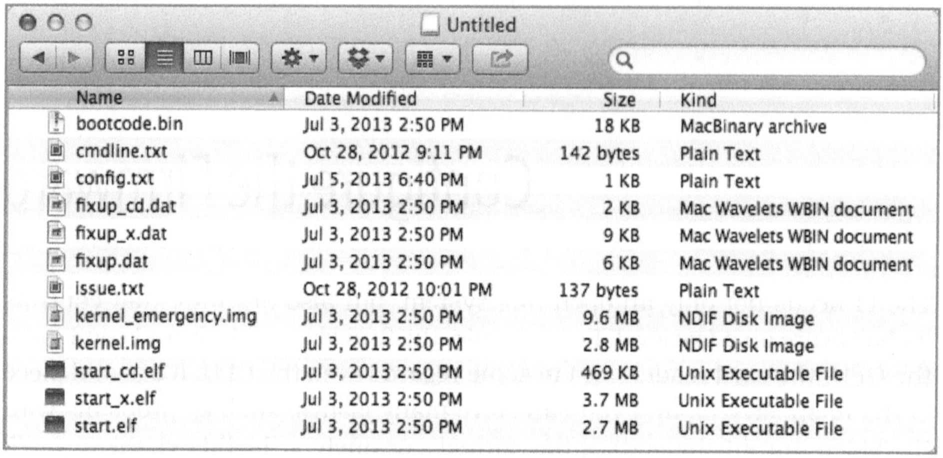

Name	Date Modified	Size	Kind
bootcode.bin	Jul 3, 2013 2:50 PM	18 KB	MacBinary archive
cmdline.txt	Oct 28, 2012 9:11 PM	142 bytes	Plain Text
config.txt	Jul 5, 2013 6:40 PM	1 KB	Plain Text
fixup_cd.dat	Jul 3, 2013 2:50 PM	2 KB	Mac Wavelets WBIN document
fixup_x.dat	Jul 3, 2013 2:50 PM	9 KB	Mac Wavelets WBIN document
fixup.dat	Jul 3, 2013 2:50 PM	6 KB	Mac Wavelets WBIN document
issue.txt	Oct 28, 2012 10:01 PM	137 bytes	Plain Text
kernel_emergency.img	Jul 3, 2013 2:50 PM	9.6 MB	NDIF Disk Image
kernel.img	Jul 3, 2013 2:50 PM	2.8 MB	NDIF Disk Image
start_cd.elf	Jul 3, 2013 2:50 PM	469 KB	Unix Executable File
start_x.elf	Jul 3, 2013 2:50 PM	3.7 MB	Unix Executable File
start.elf	Jul 3, 2013 2:50 PM	2.7 MB	Unix Executable File

Figure 19—Contents of the boot directory

The file start.elf contains the firmware, and the kernel is in kernel.img.

So, you could download the new kernel and firmware files using your regular PC and copy them to the SD card using a card reader. However, this would still be tedious and error-prone. Fortunately, rpi-update[2] automates the whole process. It checks whether a new firmware version is available and downloads it if necessary. rpi-update comes automatically with the latest version of Raspbian.

If you have to install rpi-update yourself, you will first have to install some packages it needs.

```
pi@raspberry:~$ sudo apt-get install ca-certificates git-core
```

Then you can download rpi-update and make it executable.

```
pi@raspberry:~$ sudo wget http://goo.gl/1BOfJ -O /usr/bin/rpi-update
pi@raspberry:~$ sudo chmod +x /usr/bin/rpi-update
```

After that, run rpi-update.

```
pi@raspberrypi:~$ sudo rpi-update
```

---

2.   https://github.com/Hexxeh/rpi-update

rpi-update performs a self-update first; it checks whether a newer version of rpi-update is available. Then it checks to see whether a new firmware or a new kernel is available. If yes, it downloads all files needed, and you have to reboot the Pi to activate the new firmware. Note that rpi-update even tries to determine and keep the current memory split. In *Adjust the Pi's Memory Layout*, on page 30, you learned what a memory split is and how to configure it.

Configure the Video Output

You can configure the firmware's behavior in many ways using the /boot/config.txt file. It contains all configuration parameters for the Pi's firmware; it's a good idea to bookmark their descriptions[3] in your web browser, because sooner or later you'll probably want to tweak a few things. Using the configuration file, you can adjust video and audio output, and you can even change the CPU's clock rate.

Most of the defaults work quite well on most systems, but the video output doesn't always work properly. The main problems are overscan and underscan, especially when you're using composite video output. In the case of underscan, the video output doesn't use the whole display size, so you can see a black frame around the actual video output. In the case of overscan, the opposite happens, so you can't see the whole output because it gets clipped at the display's borders.

In Figure 20, *Overscan problems can lead to a clipped output*, on page 44, the last line isn't fully visible, for example. You can solve both problems by setting a few configuration options.

As you learned in *Update the Firmware and Kernel*, on page 41, you can access all files in the /boot directory directly from your PC. If you prefer to edit /boot/config.txt on the Pi, open it with the nano text editor or a text editor of your choice.

```
pi@raspberry:~$ sudo nano /boot/config.txt
```

To adjust the display's overscan, add these lines to the configuration file:

```
# Adjust overscan.
overscan_left=10
overscan_right=20
overscan_top=0
overscan_bottom=10
```

---

3. http://elinux.org/RPi_config.txt

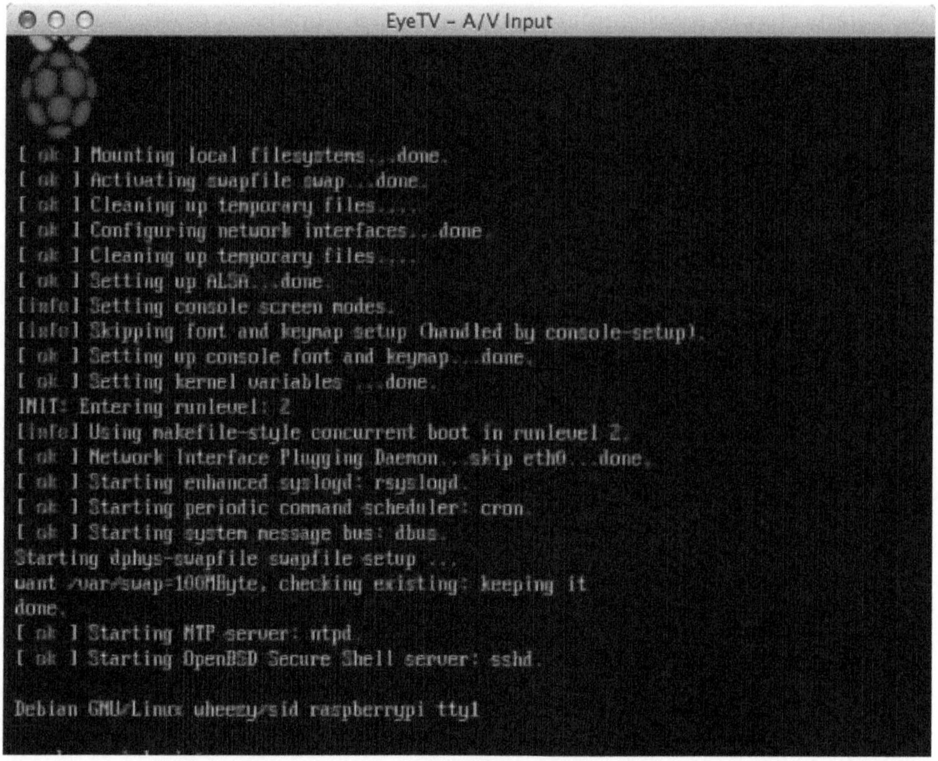

Figure 20—Overscan problems can lead to a clipped output.

Configuration parameters have a simple format: they start with a name followed by an equal sign and a value. You can also add comments to the configuration file—they start with a # character. The previous example sets the overscan_bottom option to 10 pixels so that after a reboot, the Pi will skip 10 pixels on the bottom of the display. In Figure 21, *Overscan problems can be solved easily*, on page 45, you can see the effect.

You can use the same set of options to solve underscan problems—that is, to make the display area larger and remove the black frame. To achieve this, you have to set the option values to negative numbers.

```
overscan_left=-20
overscan_right=-10
```

You have to reboot the Pi every time you change /boot/config.txt, so getting the display settings right may take a while.

It's a good idea to take a quick look at the list of all configuration parameters so you'll remember them if you run into any problems. You can play around

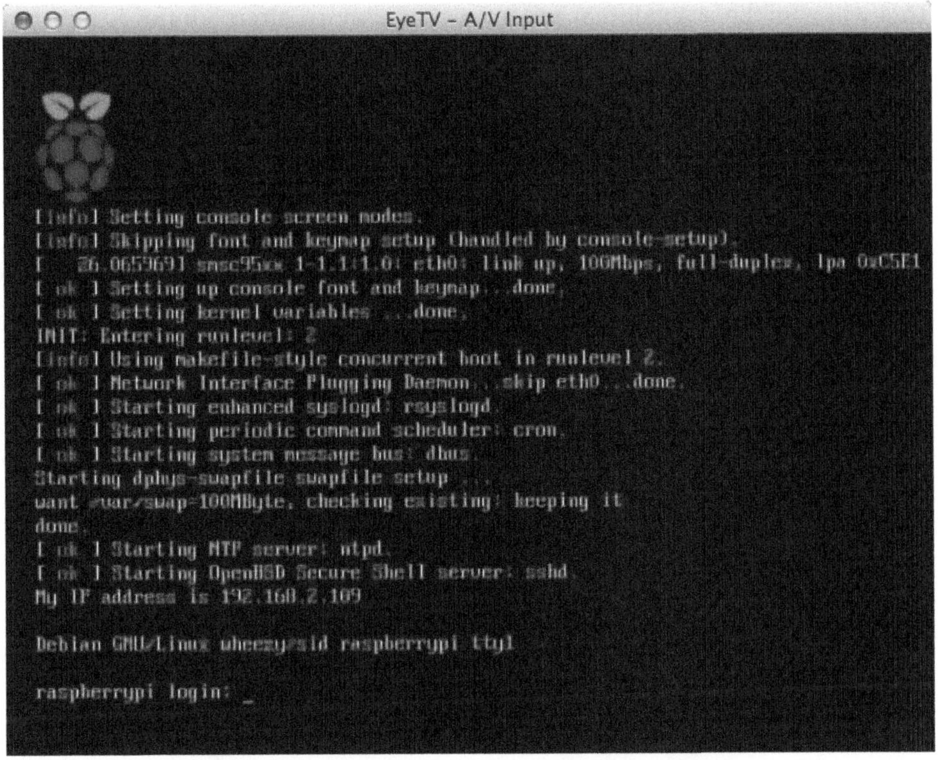

Figure 21—Overscan problems can be solved easily.

with most options, but beware: setting some options—for example, overclocking options—will void your Pi's warranty! If your Pi doesn't start any longer or if the display is no longer readable, edit /boot/config.txt on a separate PC and reverse your last changes. If you're totally lost, delete /boot/config.txt, and the Pi will start with its defaults. Of course, you can also copy a fresh Raspbian image to the SD card.

Test and Configure the Audio System

Audio output is still a bit problematic on Linux systems, but Raspbian enables audio by default. For a first sound test, run the following commands:

```
pi@raspberry:~$ cd /opt/vc/src/hello_pi/libs/ilclient
pi@raspberry:~$ make
pi@raspberry:~$ cd ../../hello_audio
pi@raspberry:~$ make
pi@raspberry:~$ ./hello_audio.bin
```

This will compile a small test program that plays a siren sound. It outputs the sound via the analog audio jack, so plug in some headphones or speakers to hear it. Alternatively, you can play the sound via HDMI.

```
pi@raspberry:~$ ./hello_audio.bin 1
```

The Pi determines the best way to output audio automatically. It uses HDMI when available and analog output otherwise. In recent versions of Raspbian, you can change this behavior using Raspi-config (see *Choose the Audio Output*, on page 30) or using amixer. This is a small tool that allows you to configure the sound hardware. Run it as follows to see which options you can change:

```
pi@raspberry:~$ amixer controls
numid=3,iface=MIXER,name='PCM Playback Route'
numid=2,iface=MIXER,name='PCM Playback Switch'
numid=1,iface=MIXER,name='PCM Playback Volume'
```

You can change only three options, and you must reference them by their *numid*. It'd be much nicer if the options had a real name, but the developers of amixer decided to use numerical IDs instead. The option for setting the playback route has a numid value of 3. Set it as follows:

```
pi@raspberry:~$ sudo amixer cset numid=3 1
```

This sets the playback route to 1 (analog output). You can also set it to 0 (automatic) or 2 (HDMI). When everything works as expected, you can add the amixer command to the /etc/rc.local file, so the Pi runs it automatically at startup. Open a text editor, such as nano, and add the following line to /etc/rc.local:

```
amixer cset numid=3 1
```

Add it to the end of the file, but don't make it the last line. Put it in front of the exit 0 statement.

By the way, some displays don't detect an HDMI cable correctly, so you might have video output via HDMI while audio output does not work. You can change this by setting the firmware configuration parameter hdmi_drive to 2 in /boot/config.txt. See *Configure the Video Output*, on page 43, to learn how to do this.

Next Steps

In this chapter, you learned how to configure the Pi's firmware. You can solve problems with the display, and you know how to adjust system parameters. In the next chapter, you'll take a short break and turn the Pi into a kiosk system.

CHAPTER 5

Intermezzo: Build a Kiosk with the Pi

If you've been in a waiting room lately, chances are good that you've seen a kiosk system.[1] Usually, it consists of an old TV set with a DVD player and sometimes even a VCR. In a doctor's waiting room, you'll see and hear a lot about new and expensive treatments, while repair shops often bombard you with advertisements for useless parts. Often the video signal flickers, the text on the show contains many typos, and you feel as if you should leave the office and look for a more professional medical provider.

On the other hand, you can find really good kiosk systems—for example, while waiting for the subway or train. Here you can see news, weather forecasts, and cartoons on huge screens. The biggest difference between the good and bad kiosks is that the good ones usually don't repeat the same content for all eternity. They often update it via the Internet.

The Raspberry Pi is a perfect platform for building a cheap but powerful kiosk system. In this chapter, you'll learn how to turn the Pi into a kiosk that displays Twitter live search information.

Display Twitter Live Search Information

The only piece of software you need to build most kiosk applications is a web browser. Web browsers are very good at displaying multimedia content, so you simply have to make the information you'd like to present available as an HTML page.

Also, you have to disable all the browser's menu bars and make sure the browser refreshes the content automatically at a certain interval. Most modern browsers already have a kiosk mode that does all of this automatically.

---

1. http://en.wikipedia.org/wiki/Kiosk_software

In Chapter 6, *Networking with the Pi*, on page 53, you'll learn a bit more about Midori, the web browser that ships with Raspbian. All in all, the browser is quite useful, and you can use it to build an impressive kiosk system.

The system you're going to build will display a live search of a list of terms on Twitter. For this book, for example, it's natural to search for the term *pragprog*. In the following screen capture, you can see the final result.

Figure 22—Results of a search for *pragprog*

The search automatically updates its content every minute. On a 46-inch screen, this system looks really impressive, and it would be a nice addition to your company's foyer.

Perhaps the screenshot reminds you of a bloated Twitter widget. This is no coincidence, because it actually is one. Usually, you'd embed such a Twitter search widget into your websites, but it is also the right technology for a kiosk system. The trick is to use the widget not as a widget but as your whole kiosk application. That way, you just have to make it really big and increase the size of your web browser's font.

One of the greatest things about widgets is that you usually don't have to create them yourself. For example, you can customize and download a Twitter search widget for free on Twitter's website.[2] You can choose the widget's title, some colors, and a search term. Then you can generate the JavaScript you need to embed the widget into your own site. The final result looks like this:

```
kiosk/widget.html
<!DOCTYPE html>
<html>
  <head>
        <meta http-equiv="refresh" content="120"></meta>
  </head>
  <body align="center">
    <a class="twitter-timeline" width="520" height="1000"
        href="https://twitter.com/search?q=%23pragprog"
        data-widget-id="357902770239594496"
        data-chrome="noscrollbar nofooter"
        data-tweet-limit="8">Tweets about "#pragprog"</a>
    <script>
        !function(d, s, id) {
                var js, fjs = d.getElementsByTagName(s)[0],
                    p = /^http:/.test(d.location) ? 'http' : 'https';
                if (!d.getElementById(id)) {
                        js = d.createElement(s);
                        js.id = id;
                        js.src = p + "://platform.twitter.com/widgets.js";
                        fjs.parentNode.insertBefore(js, fjs);
                }
        }(document, "script", "twitter-wjs");
    </script>
  </body>
</html>
```

The Twitter website generates the whole JavaScript code for you. You only have to add some boilerplate HTML. Also, the HTML code contains some style sheets to center the widget and adjust its size. Note that Twitter currently limits the widget's width to 520 pixels. You can customize a few more things, as explained on the Twitter website.[3]

Note that every Twitter widget gets a unique ID that you can see in the data-widget-id= attribute. If you want to change the search term, you have to generate a new Twitter widget with a new ID.

To get the widget code onto your Pi, you can open a text editor, such as nano, and type it in. A better approach is to download the zip archive containing the book's source code from the book's website[4] or click the filename above the preceding code example. By default, Midori stores all downloads in the /tmp directory, so after Midori has downloaded the file, open a terminal and run the following commands:

```
pi@raspberrypi ~ $ cd /tmp
pi@raspberrypi ~ $ unzip msraspi-code.zip
```

Now you can find the widget code in /tmp/code/kiosk/widget.html. To run the kiosk widget, start the LXDE desktop on your Pi, and then start the Midori browser. After that, choose the Open menu in Midori and select the file containing the widget code. The widget will start right away, but to see the full effect, press F11 to enable Midori's full-screen mode.

The widget now covers the whole screen and updates automatically. Press Ctrl++ (plus) a few times to increase the font size. Without writing a single line of code, you've turned the Pi into a kiosk system.

Refresh Websites Automatically

Many websites update their content periodically using JavaScript, and in the past Twitter widgets used this mechanism, too. The website you used in the preceding section uses a different approach. It updates its content using the <meta> tag in the head section of the HTML page.

```
<meta http-equiv="refresh" content="120"></meta>
```

This element reloads the page every 120 seconds. It's an easy solution, but it works only when you're allowed to change the page and have access to the server hosting it. So, the best solution would be if you could tell your browser to reload the current page at a certain interval. Most browsers have such a function, and usually it's called *kiosk mode*. Midori has a kiosk mode, too. To use it, you have to start Midori from the command line. Using the -a option, you specify the address Midori should display. To set the update interval, use the -i option, and to turn on full-screen mode, use -e. The final command looks like this:

---

4.   http://media.pragprog.com/titles/msraspi/code/msraspi-code.zip

```
pi@raspberrypi ~ $ midori -i 30 -e Fullscreen \
  -a "http://twitter.com/search?q=pragprog"
```

This shows the results of a Twitter search for the term *pragprog* and refreshes the page every thirty seconds. Increase the font size by hitting Ctrl++ a few times, and you're finished. Note that Midori supports many more options for controlling it from the outside. You can list them using the following command:

```
pi@raspberrypi ~ $ midori --help-execute
```

Try Different Browsers

When the Pi was released, the Midori browser was the only relatively capable browser running on the limited hardware. As the community grew, Raspbian and its applications got better and better, and now ports of Chromium and Iceweasel run fairly well on the Pi. (See *But I Want My Regular Browser*, on page 54, to learn how to install them.)

These browsers have kiosk modes, too.[5] They might provide better results for some websites than Midori does. Depending on your project's needs you might give them a try.

Next Steps

In this chapter, you learned how to turn the Pi into a kiosk system in only a few steps. Look around in your company for possible applications. For example, you could permanently display the status of your most critical systems on a big screen. Also, you could display the current number of customers or orders. Of course, you could also be conservative and simply display a set of slides explaining how wonderful your company is.

---

5. See http://www.vatofknow.com/?p=932, for example.

CHAPTER 6

Networking with the Pi

Like any computer, the Pi gets even more exciting the moment you connect it to a network. Suddenly, you can use the Pi for everyday tasks, such as surfing the Web or tweeting messages. You also can make the Pi accessible via Secure Shell, so you can securely and conveniently work on it from another computer. You can even share the Pi's graphical desktop with your PC over a network, and vice versa.

In addition, you can use the Pi as a cheap but powerful web server that not only serves static content, but also is able to run web applications written in languages such as PHP, for example.

Perform Everyday Tasks on the Web

You're probably used to performing many tasks using only your web browser: checking email, reading RSS feeds, watching videos, sending tweets, and so on. This is all possible because most browsers today support HTML5, JavaScript, Flash, and Java. Without these technologies, the Web would still look very much like it did in 1995.

All these nice things work only with modern browsers, such as Google Chrome or Mozilla Firefox. Although you can already install Chromium on Raspbian,[1] it will be a while until it will run sufficiently fast on the Pi. Also, it doesn't support all features, such as video, at the moment. The biggest limitation is due to the Pi's small memory, because modern browsers use a lot of it. The browser that ships with the Debian distribution for the Pi is Midori.[2] It's a pretty good web browser that doesn't use a lot of memory. Unfortunately, it's still in its infancy, and it has some limitations. For one thing, technologies

---

1. http://hexxeh.net/?p=328117859
2. http://twotoasts.de/index.php/midori/

such as Flash and Java aren't currently available on the Pi. So, if you come across a website that uses Flash or a Java applet, it won't work in any browser running on the Pi.

But I Want My Regular Browser

The basis of the Google Chrome browser is the Chromium project.[a] There is no Google Chrome for the Raspberry Pi, but at least you can run the Chromium browser. As of this writing, the Chromium port is rather slow, but if you still want to install Chromium on the Pi, run the following command:

```
pi@raspberrypi ~ $ sudo apt-get install chromium
```

Then you can start Chromium from a terminal on the LXDE desktop using the following command:

```
pi@raspberrypi ~ $ chromium
```

You'll also find a shortcut to the Chromium browser in the application menu. To make it run as fast as possible, devote a maximum of 32MB of RAM to the GPU (see *Adjust the Pi's Memory Layout*, on page 30). Also, you should consider overclocking your Pi (see *Accelerate/Overclock the Pi*, on page 29).

Similarly, you can install Iceweasel, a Firefox port for Debian.[b]

```
pi@raspberrypi ~ $ sudo apt-get install iceweasel
```

Afterwards, you'll find a shortcut to the Iceweasel browser in the Internet section of the application menu. As with Chromium, you'll get better performance by overclocking your Pi.

---

a. http://www.chromium.org/
b. http://en.wikipedia.org/wiki/Mozilla_Corporation_software_rebranded_by_the_Debian_project#IceWeasel

---

Although Midori understands HTML5, CSS3, and JavaScript, it's not capable of properly interpreting all modern websites. For example, not all features of Google Mail run out of the box, because Midori doesn't understand some of the site's JavaScript. Also, Midori needs some time to render Google Mail's default view. You can improve this situation by disabling JavaScript using Midori's Preferences > Behaviour menu and by choosing Google Mail's basic HTML view.

Disabling JavaScript can improve the usability of other websites, too. When you disable JavaScript in your browser, many websites will return a plain HTML version of their service. This HTML version usually doesn't have all the bells and whistles of the original site, but at least you can use it.

For Twitter, it's similar. Midori can render it, but it's rather slow. A good solution is to use Twitter's mobile website.[3] It won't have all the features of the original site, but it will still provide a very good Twitter experience, and it works on Midori.

Another trick that sometimes helps is to change Midori's user agent. All web browsers send with every request a unique identifier that tells the web server exactly what kind of browser has sent the request. This identifier is called the *user agent*, and some websites change their response depending on its value. For example, some websites generate an error message if they don't know the user agent. In Midori, you can change the user agent in the Preferences > Network menu. Here you can tell Midori that it should pretend to be a Mozilla Firefox browser, Safari, or an iPhone.

Some sites won't work at the moment, no matter what you try. YouTube,[4] for example, depends on video support in the browser, be it HTML5 video or Flash. Midori doesn't support either of these on Raspbian at the moment, so you can't render YouTube properly. You're out of luck, too, if a website depends on some JavaScript code that doesn't work on Midori or if it needs a Java applet. Fortunately, Java applets aren't very popular today, but some online banking sites still use them.

In addition to all this, Midori sometimes uses a lot of resources, especially the CPU. Midori often needs nearly the whole CPU to render a website—sometimes you have to wait for a few minutes for just one page to render.

A Glimpse into the Future

The Raspberry Pi team has always known that the lack of a really good web browser is one of the platform's biggest problems. Instead of waiting for someone else to come up with a decent solution, they've tried to improve the situation—chances are good now that the Pi will eventually get a really good web browser.[a]

This browser is named "Web" (admittedly not the most creative name for a web browser), and it has been around for quite a long time.[b] At the moment, early beta ports for the Pi are available, and they look quite promising.

a.   http://www.raspberrypi.org/archives/5535
b.   http://en.wikipedia.org/wiki/Web_%28web_browser%29

3.   http://mobile.twitter.com
4.   http://youtube.com

If you keep in mind that you can disable JavaScript and that most popular websites have a mobile version, Midori is sufficient for most situations. Also, the Pi's popularity might result in major improvements in the near future.

Use Secure Shell with the Pi

It's likely that you'll connect your Pi to a network so you can access the Pi from other computers, and vice versa. One of the best ways to communicate securely between two computers is via *Secure Shell* (SSH), a network protocol for secure data communication. Debian comes with everything you need to use SSH; you simply have to configure a few things.

Access the Pi Using a Password

If you only want to access other computers from the Pi, you don't have to configure anything. For example, you can connect as the admin user to the host maik-schmidt.de by starting SSH on the Pi with the other computer's name and password.

```
pi@raspberrypi ~ $ ssh admin@maik-schmidt.de
admin@maik-schmidt.de's password:
Last login: Wed Jan  2 09:41:34 2013 from 94.221.82.250
admin@maik-schmidt.de:~$ exit
logout
Connection to maik-schmidt.de closed.
```

However, if you want to access the Pi using SSH, you first have to enable the SSH server on the Pi using Raspi-config.

```
pi@raspberrypi ~ $ sudo raspi-config
```

Choose the SSH menu item in the Advanced Options menu and enable the SSH server. Then click the Finish button to leave Raspi-config. After you reboot, the Pi's boot log will contain a new message.

```
Starting OpenBSD Secure Shell server: sshd
My IP address is 192.168.2.109
```

This means you can access the Pi via SSH now, and that the Pi's IP address is 192.168.2.109. In your case, the IP address will likely be different. If you need to determine your Pi's IP address later, you can run this:

```
pi@raspberrypi ~ $ ip addr | grep 'inet .* eth0'
inet 192.168.2.109/24 brd 192.168.2.255 scope global eth0
```

The first IP address that appears in the output is your Pi's address. Using this address, you can access the Pi from all the other computers on your network.

From a Mac or a Linux system, you can start SSH from the command line, passing it the Pi user's IP address and password.

```
maik> ssh pi@192.168.2.109
pi@192.168.2.109's password:
Linux raspberrypi 3.10.25+ #622 PREEMPT Fri Jan 3 18:41:00 GMT 2014 armv6l

The programs included with the Debian GNU/Linux system are free software;
the exact distribution terms for each program are described in the
individual files in /usr/share/doc/*/copyright.

Debian GNU/Linux comes with ABSOLUTELY NO WARRANTY, to the extent
permitted by applicable law.
Last login: Tue Feb  4 20:55:56 2014
pi@raspberrypi ~ $ exit
logout
Connection to 192.168.2.109 closed.
```

To access the Pi from a Windows box, you need an SSH client, and one of the best is PuTTY.[5] It's a very small program that you don't even have to install. Download the executable, start it, and you'll see the configuration screen shown in Figure 23, *PuTTY configuration screen*, on page 58.

PuTTY allows you to configure many things, and it lets you store your configuration for each type of session you need. To log into the Pi, you simply enter its IP address and click the Open button. Then you'll see the Pi's regular login prompt, as in Figure 24, *Accessing the Pi from Windows is easy*, on page 58.

Access the Pi with a Public-Private Key Pair

If you often have to access your Pi via SSH, it might get tedious to always enter the password when you log in. A more convenient method is to use the public-private key mechanism. To do that, you have to generate a key on your PC. The key has two parts, one private and one public, and you copy the public part to the Pi. The next time you log in to the Pi from your PC, SSH will verify your identity by checking whether the public and private parts of the key match. If you want to access the Pi from several computers, you have to run the steps in this section for each of them.

Before you generate a new key pair, you should check to see whether you have one already. On Linux or Mac OS X, open a terminal and run the following command:

```
maik> ls ~/.ssh/id_rsa.pub
/Users/maik/.ssh/id_rsa.pub
```

---

5. http://www.chiark.greenend.org.uk/~sgtatham/putty/download.html

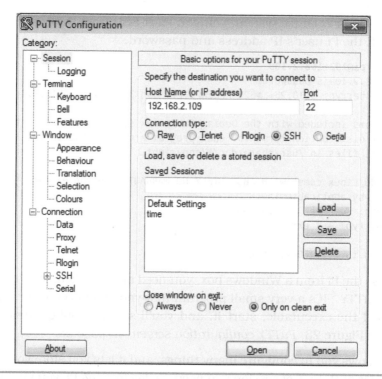

Figure 23—PuTTY configuration screen

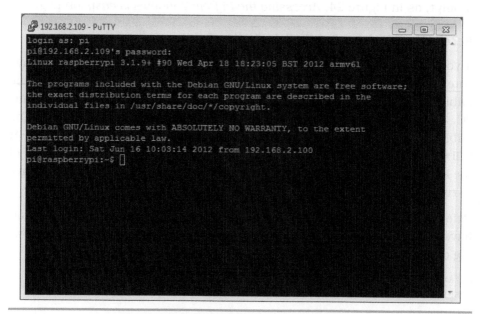

Figure 24—Accessing the Pi from Windows is easy.

The file id_rsa.pub contains the public key, and the command shown earlier tries to list it. If the output looks like the previous output, you already have a key, and you can skip the key generation and copy the public key to the Pi, as described next. If you get a "No such file or directory" message instead, you have to generate a key, as in the following:

```
maik> ssh-keygen -t rsa -C "your_email@youremail.com"
Generating public-private rsa key pair.
Enter file in which to save the key (/Users/maik/.ssh/id_rsa):
Enter passphrase (empty for no passphrase):
Enter same passphrase again:
Your identification has been saved in
/Users/mschmidt/.ssh/id_rsa.
Your public key has been saved in
/Users/mschmidt/.ssh/id_rsa.pub.
The key fingerprint is:
f0:09:09:49:42:46:42:6f:42:3b:42:44:42:09:6a:e8
your_email@youremail.com
The key's randomart image is:
+--[ RSA 2048]----+
| . .o..          |
|+  ..o + .       |
|o.o + B o        |
|.+ o o B .       |
| E   = S .       |
| .   . o         |
|       .         |
|                 |
|                 |
+-----------------+
```

This generated a key pair in your home directory. You can find the public key in a file named id_rsa.pub. You now have to transfer this file to the Pi, where SSH keeps a list of all authorized keys in a file named .ssh/authorized_keys in the Pi user's home directory. The following commands append the id_rsa.pub file to the Pi's list of authorized keys:

```
maik> scp ~/.ssh/id_rsa.pub pi@192.168.2.109:/tmp
maik> ssh pi@192.168.2.109 "mkdir ~/.ssh"
maik> ssh pi@192.168.2.109 "cat /tmp/id_rsa.pub >> ~/.ssh/authorized_keys"
```

The first command copies id_rsa.pub to the Pi's /tmp directory, and the second command creates a hidden directory named .ssh that contains configuration data for SSH. The last command appends the file's content to the ~/.ssh/authorized_keys file. If you don't plan to keep several keys in the authorized_keys file, you can copy id_rsa.pub directly, of course.

```
maik> scp ~/.ssh/id_rsa.pub pi@192.168.2.109:/home/pi/.ssh/authorized_keys
```

On a Windows box, you can use some additional tools from the PuTTY download page to generate the keys and to copy them to the Pi. In the following figure you can see the PuTTYgen application that generates keys.

Figure 25—PuTTYgen generates keys on Windows.

To copy the generated public key file, use PSCP. It works exactly like scp, so from a DOS prompt, run the following command:

```
C:\> pscp id_rsa.pub pi@192.168.2.109:/home/pi/.ssh/authorized_keys
```

Your Pi is a full-fledged member of your network now.

Share Desktops with the Pi

Logging into the Pi using SSH is convenient and opens a new world of possibilities. For example, you can access the Pi's file system, start and stop processes, and monitor what's happening on the Pi at the moment. The biggest disadvantage of the SSH solution so far is that it only works in a text terminal.

You can easily overcome this limitation and control the Pi's desktop, keyboard, and mouse using another computer. One solution is Virtual Network Computing (VNC),[6] a technology that transmits the whole screen and all mouse and keyboard events from one computer to another.

To enable VNC, you need a VNC client and server. The server runs on the machine you'd like to control, and the client runs on the controlling machine. So, if you want to control the Pi using your PC, you have to install a VNC server on your Pi. You can choose from several, but one of the best is TightVNC.[7] It's available for free for all major platforms, and you can install it via apt-get.

```
pi@raspberrypi ~ $ sudo apt-get install tightvncserver
pi@raspberrypi ~ $ tightvncserver

You will require a password to access your desktops.

Password:
Verify:
Would you like to enter a view-only password (y/n)? n

New 'X' desktop is raspberrypi:1

Creating default startup script /home/pi/.vnc/xstartup
Starting applications specified in /home/pi/.vnc/xstartup
Log file is /home/pi/.vnc/raspberrypi:1.log
```

When you run tightvncserver for the first time, it asks you to set a password. You have to enter this password in the VNC client later to prevent unauthorized people from accessing your Pi. In addition, TightVNC allows you to optionally define a view-only password. This password gives clients read-only access so they can see the screen, but they cannot control the keyboard and mouse. This is useful for presentations, for example.

After you've defined the passwords, TightVNC creates a new virtual screen that you can access from your PC or Mac. The great thing about VNC is that it allows you to create as many virtual screens as you need. These screens don't necessarily have to correspond to physical screens. They are purely virtual, so many users can access your Pi, for example, and each will get an independent desktop environment.

To address a virtual screen, you need two things: the Pi's IP address and the screen's port address. VNC's base port is 5900, so to access screen number 1,

---

6.　http://en.wikipedia.org/wiki/Vnc

7.　http://www.tightvnc.com/

you have to use port 5901. To access the screen you've created with the previous commands, you have to use the network address 192.168.2.109:5901. Keep in mind that your IP address will probably be different.

Now that you know the address of the Pi's VNC server, you can access it from a PC or a Mac using a VNC client. On a Mac it's very easy, because the Mac comes with a VNC client already. You can actually connect to a VNC server using the Safari web browser. Simply enter the web address vnc://192.168.2.109:5901, and Safari will spawn the Screen Sharing application. Enter the password you defined earlier, and you're finished. See the result in the following figure.

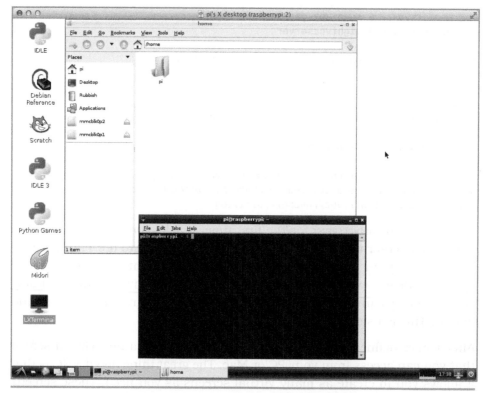

Figure 26—Controlling the Pi from a Mac

On Windows and Linux, the procedure is very similar, but you have to install a VNC client first. This is easy, because TightVNC runs on Windows and Linux, and it contains a client, too.

Controlling your PC's or Mac's desktop from the Pi is easy, too. First you have to install a VNC server on your PC. Again, TightVNC is a great choice for

Windows and Linux. On a Mac it's even easier, because Mac OS X has an integrated VNC server that you simply have to enable. In the System Preferences, select Sharing and then enable Screen Sharing. Click the Computer Settings button to set a password. (You can see the preferences panel in the following figure.)

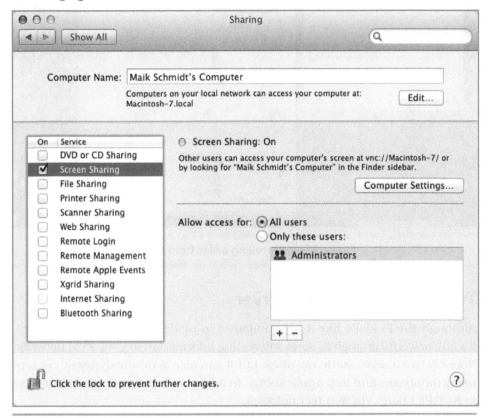

Figure 27—Sharing the Mac's screen is easy.

Now you need a VNC client on the Pi, and xtightvncviewer is a good one. Install it using apt-get.

```
pi@raspberrypi ~ $ sudo apt-get install xtightvncviewer
```

Then open a terminal on the Pi's desktop and start the client, passing it your PC's IP address and VNC port.

```
pi@raspberrypi ~ $ xtightvncviewer 192.168.2.100:5900
```

In Figure 28, *Controlling a Mac from the Pi*, on page 64, you can see a Mac's desktop inside a window on the Pi's desktop. If it doesn't work, make sure you use the correct IP address and port number. Usually it's 5900, but it might vary in different VNC servers.

Figure 28—Controlling a Mac from the Pi

Turn the Pi into a Web Server

Although the Pi looks like a toy compared to modern web server hardware, it's still powerful enough to serve interesting information in your local network. Not only can it serve static websites, but it can also generate dynamic content using databases and web applications. In addition, it can even provide access to its GPIO ports via web technologies.

The first thing you need to turn the Pi into a web server is an HTTP server, a network service that understands the Hypertext Transfer Protocol (HTTP). You can choose from several great products, such as the Apache HTTP server[8] or Nginx,[9] but Lighttpd[10] is a good choice for the Pi because of its very low memory footprint.

Installing/running Lighttpd is a piece of cake.

```
pi@raspberrypi ~ $ sudo apt-get install lighttpd
```

---

8. http://httpd.apache.org/
9. http://nginx.org/
10. http://www.lighttpd.net/

After the installation has completed, Lighttpd is up and running, and you can point your PC's web browser to your Pi's IP address. For example, in the following figure you can see the server's welcome page.

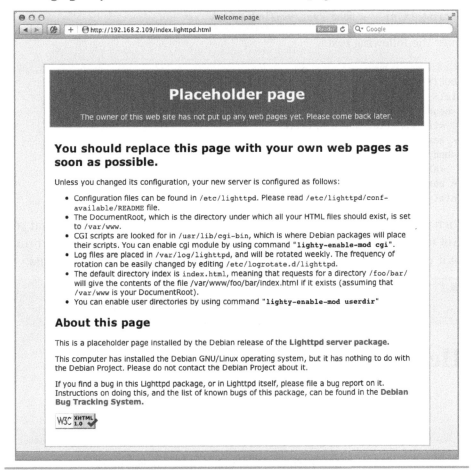

Figure 29—Lighttpd's welcome page

To create your own web pages, you have to add them to Lighttpd's document root, a directory containing all files it should serve for a website. Lighttpd's document root by default is the /var/www directory. You should make sure that only members of the operating system group www-data have permission to write to it. The following commands add a Pi user to the www-data group and set the permission flags of the /var/www directory accordingly:

```
pi@raspberrypi ~ $ sudo adduser pi www-data
pi@raspberrypi ~ $ sudo chown -R www-data:www-data /var/www
pi@raspberrypi ~ $ sudo chmod -R 775 /var/www
```

After the next login, you can create new web pages. You can do it with any text editor, such as nano. The following command creates a new file named index.html that will be the start page of your first website:

pi@raspberrypi ~ $ **nano /var/www/index.html**

Enter the following text:

```
Networking/index.html
<!DOCTYPE html>
<html>
  <head>
    <title>Hello, world!</title>
  </head>
  <body>
    <h1>Hello, world!</h1>
  </body>
</html>
```

When you're finished, press Ctrl+X to leave nano. Press Y to confirm that you want to save the file, and then press Enter to confirm the filename. After that, point your browser to the new web page, and you'll see a result like this:

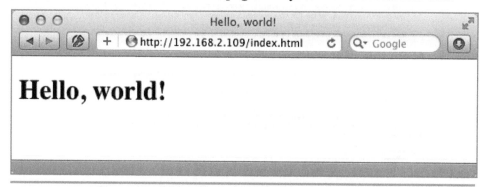

Figure 30—Results of pointing to the new web page

By the way, if you prefer, you can edit the index.html file on your PC and copy it to the Pi afterward. (Remember to replace the IP address with your Pi's IP address.)

maik> **scp index.html pi@192.168.2.109:/var/www**

Using only a few commands, you've turned the Pi into a full-blown web server that can serve static content, such as HTML pages. This is useful, but sometimes you need more dynamic content. For example, you might want to embed data from a database into your pages, or you might even embed environmental data you collect with sensors attached to the Pi.

To create dynamic content, you need a programming language. You can choose from many alternatives. For the Pi, PHP[11] is a good choice because it doesn't use a lot of resources and it's easy to install.

```
pi@raspberrypi ~ $ sudo apt-get update
pi@raspberrypi ~ $ sudo apt-get install php5-cgi
pi@raspberrypi ~ $ sudo lighty-enable-mod fastcgi-php
pi@raspberrypi ~ $ sudo /etc/init.d/lighttpd force-reload
```

These commands install a PHP interpreter and enable the FastCGI module in the Lighttpd server. FastCGI[12] speeds up dynamic websites tremendously, so it's a good idea to enable it.

To test whether everything works as expected, create a file named /var/www/index.php with the following content:

Networking/index.php
```
<?php
  phpinfo();
?>
```

Point your web browser to the newly created file, and you should see something similar to Figure 31, *Serving dynamic web pages from the Pi*, on page 68.

This is PHP's info page, which contains a lot of information about the system on which PHP is currently running. PHP generates it dynamically. You can see that everything works fine, and now you can start to build your own web applications on the Pi. In Chapter 9, *Tinker with the GPIO Pins*, on page 93, you'll build a web application that controls some external hardware attached to the Pi.

Add Wi-Fi to the Pi

Wireless networks are everywhere these days. Coffee shops, airports, and hotels generally offer Wi-Fi to their customers. You probably run a wireless network at home, too, so you can conveniently access your most important services from your smartphone while you're having a barbecue with the family. On Windows or Mac OS X, you usually don't have to think much about joining wireless networks because the process is nearly invisible.

On the Pi it's different, because the Pi's hardware doesn't support Wi-Fi by default. You need a Wi-Fi stick for the USB port, and depending on the stick's type, Raspbian might configure it automatically. In some cases you have to configure it manually; in this section, you'll learn both ways.

---

11. http://www.php.net/
12. http://www.fastcgi.com/

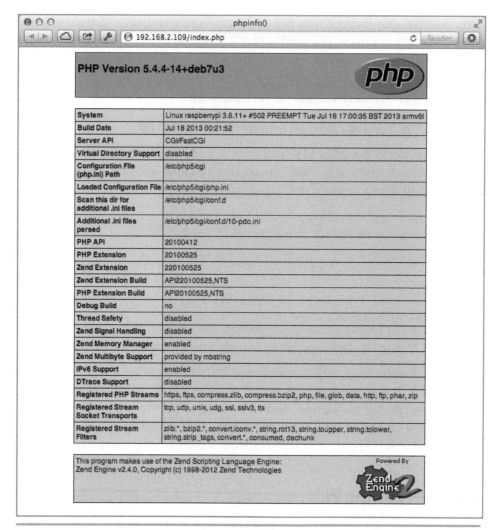

Figure 31—Serving dynamic web pages from the Pi

Configure Wi-Fi Using WiFi Config

The easiest way to configure Wi-Fi on Raspbian is to use a graphical tool named WiFi Config. Plug the Wi-Fi stick into a USB port and start the LXDE desktop:

```
pi@raspberrypi ~ $ startx
```

On the desktop you'll find an icon for WiFi Config. Double-click it, and you'll see the application shown in Figure 32, *WiFi Config lets you scan for wireless networks,* on page 69.

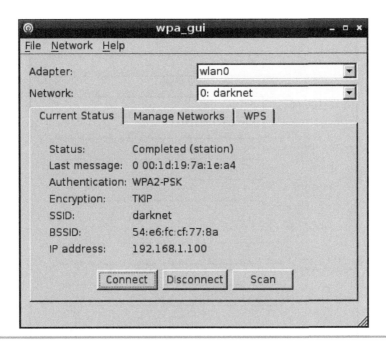

Figure 32—WiFi Config lets you scan for wireless networks.

Choose wlan0 from the Adapter drop-down menu and then click the Scan button to search for wireless networks. If you find the network you've been looking for, double-click its name, and the configuration dialog in Figure 33, *You can change many parameters in WiFi Config*, on page 70 will appear.

Usually, you don't have to change anything here. You only have to enter your Wi-Fi password in the PSK text field. Press the Save button to return to the main menu and then press the Connect button to connect the Pi to the wireless network. If everything works as expected, save the current configuration using the File > Save Configuration menu.

As long as Raspbian and WiFi Config recognize your Wi-Fi stick, WiFi Config is the most convenient way to join wireless networks with the Pi. Unfortunately, WiFi Config doesn't work with all Wi-Fi sticks, and sometimes you might need to avoid the desktop system because you're running a server. In these cases you have to configure Wi-Fi manually.

Configure Wi-Fi Manually

Configuring Wi-Fi on the command line isn't very convenient, but it isn't rocket science, either. Plug your Wi-Fi stick into one of the Pi's USB ports and run the lsusb command to see whether the Pi recognizes it properly:

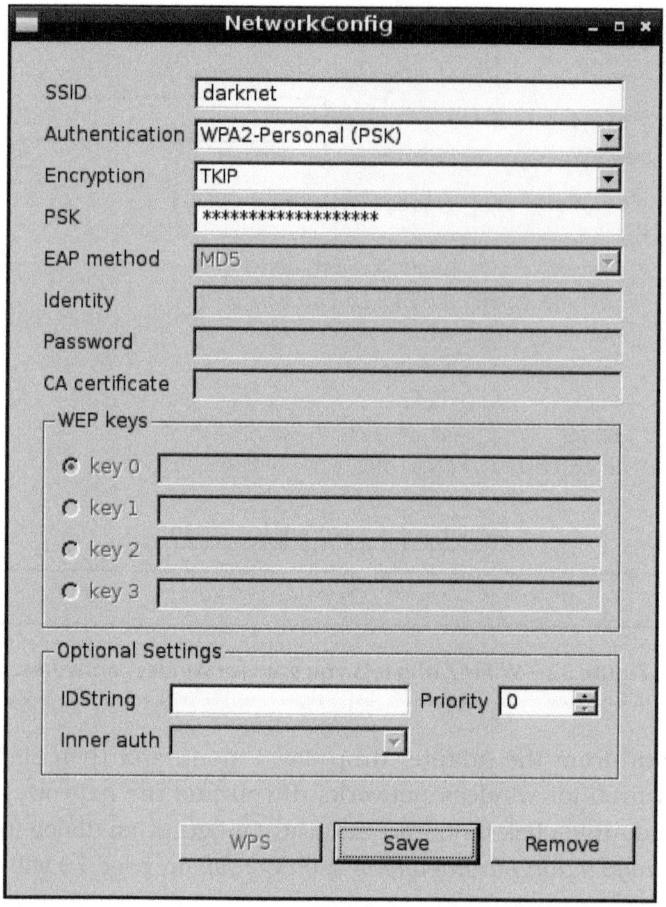

Figure 33—You can change many parameters in WiFi Config.

```
pi@raspberrypi ~ $ lsusb
Bus 001 Device 001: ID 1d6b:0002 Linux Foundation 2.0 root hub
Bus 001 Device 002: ID 0424:9512 Standard Microsystems Corp.
Bus 001 Device 003: ID 0424:ec00 Standard Microsystems Corp.
Bus 001 Device 004: ID 050d:0237 Belkin Components F5U237 USB 2.0 7-Port Hub
Bus 001 Device 005: ID 04e8:2018 Samsung Electronics Co., Ltd WIS09ABGN
                                 LinkStick Wireless LAN Adapter
Bus 001 Device 006: ID 046d:c312 Logitech, Inc. DeLuxe 250 Keyboard
Bus 001 Device 007: ID 046d:c05a Logitech, Inc. Optical Mouse M90
```

In this case, device 005 is a Wi-Fi stick manufactured by Samsung. You can take a closer look at the Pi's boot message with the dmesg command and see whether the WLAN stick has been initialized properly:

```
pi@raspberrypi ~ $ dmesg | less
...
usb 1-1.3.6: new high speed USB device number 5 using dwc_otg
usb 1-1.3.6: New USB device found, idVendor=04e8, idProduct=2018
usb 1-1.3.6: New USB device strings: Mfr=1, Product=2, SerialNumber=3
usb 1-1.3.6: Product: 802.11 n WLAN
usb 1-1.3.6: Manufacturer: Ralink
usb 1-1.3.6: SerialNumber: 1.0
...
```

Press the spacebar to go down one page and press B to go up one page. Press Q to go back to the shell prompt. As you can see in the current case, the Samsung stick uses the Wi-Fi chipset from a company named Ralink. This chipset is pretty popular, so Debian recognized it out of the box. If the output of dmesg contains any errors right after the initialization of your Wi-Fi stick, check the Pi's wiki.[13] Often you have to download the firmware for your Wi-Fi stick manually and reconfigure the Linux kernel.

If no errors occurred, Debian Linux has recognized your Wi-Fi stick successfully. You can use the following command to get the current status of your Pi's wireless network interfaces:

```
pi@raspberrypi ~ $ iwconfig
lo        no wireless extensions.

eth0      no wireless extensions.

wlan0     IEEE 802.11abgn  ESSID:off/any
          Mode:Managed  Access Point: Not-Associated   Tx-Power=20 dBm
          Retry  long limit:7   RTS thr:off   Fragment thr:off
          Power Management:on
```

At the moment, the Pi isn't connected to a wireless network, but the wlan0 interface is up and running. The following command searches for wireless networks:

```
pi@raspberrypi ~ $ sudo iwlist scan | grep ESSID
        ESSID:"darknet"
        ESSID:"valhalla"
```

In this case, two wireless networks named darknet and valhalla are within reach. To connect to one of them, you have to edit the configuration file /etc/network/interfaces using a text editor, such as nano. The configuration file should look like this after editing:

13. http://elinux.org/RPi_VerifiedPeripherals#USB_WiFi_Adapters

```
auto lo
iface lo inet loopback
iface eth0 inet dhcp

allow-hotplug wlan0
iface wlan0 inet manual
wpa-roam /etc/wpa_supplicant/wpa_supplicant.conf
iface default inet dhcp
```

These lines will activate the wlan0 network interface automatically the next time you boot the Pi without an Ethernet connection. Also, they'll make the Pi obtain an IP address using DHCP (Dynamic Host Configuration Protocol).

You still have to configure your Wi-Fi credentials. Open /etc/wpa_supplicant/wpa_supplicant.conf with your text editor of choice and enter the following lines:

```
ctrl_interface=DIR=/var/run/wpa_supplicant GROUP=netdev
update_config=1

network={
    ssid="darknet"
    psk="dontTellAny0ne"
    proto=RSN
    key_mgmt=WPA-PSK
    pairwise=TKIP
    auth_alg=OPEN
}
```

Of course, you have to adjust the parameters ssid and psk accordingly.

If you're impatient, you don't have to reboot the Pi. Run the following command to make the Pi join your wireless network:

```
pi@raspberrypi ~ $ sudo ifup wlan0
Internet Systems Consortium DHCP Client 4.2.2
Copyright 2004-2011 Internet Systems Consortium.
All rights reserved.
For info, please visit https://www.isc.org/software/dhcp/

Listening on LPF/wlan0/00:12:fb:28:a9:51
Sending on   LPF/wlan0/00:12:fb:28:a9:51
Sending on   Socket/fallback
DHCPDISCOVER on wlan0 to 255.255.255.255 port 67 interval 8
DHCPDISCOVER on wlan0 to 255.255.255.255 port 67 interval 14
DHCPDISCOVER on wlan0 to 255.255.255.255 port 67 interval 14
DHCPREQUEST on wlan0 to 255.255.255.255 port 67
DHCPOFFER from 192.168.1.1
DHCPACK from 192.168.1.1
bound to 192.168.1.101 -- renewal in 2983 seconds.
```

The Pi has the IP address 192.168.1.101 now and is connected to your network wirelessly. (Your IP address probably will differ.) Use the ping command to check whether you can access a website such as Google, for example:

```
pi@raspberrypi ~ $ ping -c 3 google.com
PING google.com (173.194.69.100) 56(84) bytes of data.
64 bytes from google.com (173.194.69.100): icmp_req=1 ttl=45 time=26.7 ms
64 bytes from google.com (173.194.69.100): icmp_req=2 ttl=45 time=32.3 ms
64 bytes from google.com (173.194.69.100): icmp_req=3 ttl=45 time=34.8 ms

--- google.com ping statistics ---
3 packets transmitted, 3 received, 0% packet loss, time 2002ms
rtt min/avg/max/mdev = 26.752/31.338/34.863/3.395 ms
```

As you can see, the Pi is connected to the Internet via Wi-Fi now. Run the following command to get some statistics about the signal strength and so on:

```
pi@raspberrypi ~ $ iwconfig
lo        no wireless extensions.

eth0      no wireless extensions.

wlan0     IEEE 802.11abgn  ESSID:"darknet"
          Mode:Managed  Frequency:2.442 GHz  Access Point: 54:E6:FC:CF:77:8A
          Bit Rate=135 Mb/s    Tx-Power=20 dBm
          Retry  long limit:7   RTS thr:off   Fragment thr:off
          Power Management:on
          Link Quality=40/70  Signal level=-70 dBm
          Rx invalid nwid:0  Rx invalid crypt:0  Rx invalid frag:0
          Tx excessive retries:1  Invalid misc:6   Missed beacon:0
```

Keep in mind that a computer like the Pi can have more than one IP address. If you connect it via Ethernet and Wi-Fi, for example, your boot message will display something like the following:

```
My IP address is 192.168.2.109 192.168.1.101
```

That means that you've connected your Pi using two network interfaces, and for each interface it has a different IP address.

Configure Static IP Addresses

Until now you've configured all network devices using DHCP. That is, your router assigns an IP address to your Pi automatically. This IP address is unique, but it might change. In some cases it's more convenient to assign a static IP address—that is, an IP address that always stays the same. Of course, you have to make sure you don't use an IP address that is being used by another device in your network.

Configuring static IP addresses isn't much different from configuring dynamic IP addresses. You have to edit /etc/network/interfaces first. The following file assigns a dynamic IP address to the Ethernet device. Also, it assigns the static IP address 192.168.1.105 to the Wi-Fi device:

```
auto lo
iface lo inet loopback
iface eth0 inet dhcp

allow-hotplug wlan0
iface wlan0 inet manual
wpa-roam /etc/wpa_supplicant/wpa_supplicant.conf

iface home inet static
address 192.168.1.105
netmask 255.255.255.0
network 192.168.1.0
gateway 192.168.1.1
```

Make sure you're using the correct addresses for netmask, network, and gateway. Also, make sure the address 192.168.1.105 isn't used by any other device on your wireless network.

In this case, the static interface's name is "home." You have to connect it to the Wi-Fi credentials by changing /etc/wpa_supplicant/wpa_supplicant.conf slightly:

```
ctrl_interface=DIR=/var/run/wpa_supplicant GROUP=netdev
update_config=1

network={
  ssid="darknet"
  psk="t0p$ecret"
  proto=RSN
  key_mgmt=WPA-PSK
  pairwise=TKIP
  auth_alg=OPEN
  id_str="home"
}
```

The only thing you have to add is id_str="home". After you reboot the Pi, it will listen on a dynamic Ethernet address and a static wireless address.

Next Steps

In this chapter, you learned how to integrate the Pi into your network. You can now conveniently access the Pi via SSH, and you can even use it as a web server. In the next chapter, you'll do something completely different: you'll turn the Pi into a multimedia center.

CHAPTER 7

Turn the Pi into a Multimedia Center

The Pi's small size, its low power consumption, and its graphics capabilities make it a perfect candidate for a fully integrated multimedia center, just like a PlayStation or an Apple TV box. To turn the Pi into such a multimedia center, you need a special piece of software named XBMC.[1]

XBMC is a media player on steroids that can turn nearly every PC into an entertainment hub for digital media. The Pi is no exception. In this chapter, you'll learn how to run XBMC on the Pi.

Install Raspbmc

XBMC is a really big software project, and installing and configuring it can be tricky. Fortunately, you don't have to do it yourself for the Pi; you can benefit from the glorious efforts of the Raspbmc[2] team. Raspbmc is a Linux distribution for the Pi that does nothing but run XBMC. You can install it using NOOBS (see *Have a Look Around with NOOBS*, on page 14) or copy an image of this distribution to an SD card as usual. Then you can use the SD card to boot the Pi. Instead of starting a terminal or a desktop environment, the Raspbmc distribution starts XBMC automatically.

In contrast to other Linux distributions for the Pi, the Raspbmc team not only offers for download a complete image file for an SD card, they also decided to create an installer for all major platforms. This installer downloads the latest version of Raspbmc from the Web and automatically copies it to your SD card.

---

1. http://xbmc.org/
2. http://www.raspbmc.com/

If you're using a Windows PC to prepare a Raspbmc card, download the installer,[3] extract it to your hard drive, and start the program named installer.exe. You'll see a window similar to this:

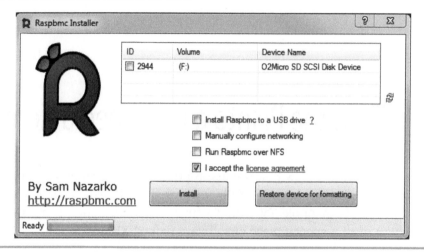

Figure 34—Raspbmc installer for Windows

Insert an SD card, select your SD card reader, and click the Install button. The installer will download the latest version of Raspbmc and copy it to the SD card. Note that the installer will delete all the data on the SD card.

The Raspbmc installer for Linux and Mac OS X doesn't have a fancy UI, but it's easy to use. It's a Python program, and after you've downloaded it,[4] you can run it from a terminal, as in the following example:

```
maik> sudo python install.py

< Raspbmc installer for Linux and OS X
  http://raspbmc.com
  ----------------------------------------
  Please ensure you've inserted your SD card, and press Enter to continue.

  Enter the 'IDENTIFIER' of the device you would like imaged:
    #:                TYPE NAME              SIZE        IDENTIFIER
    0:      GUID_partition_scheme          *256.1 GB    disk0
    0:      GUID_partition_scheme          *500.1 GB    disk1
    0:      FDisk_partition_scheme         *500.1 GB    disk2
    0:      FDisk_partition_scheme         *1.0 TB      disk3
    0:      FDisk_partition_scheme         *2.0 GB      disk4
    0:      GUID_partition_scheme          *1.5 TB      disk5
```

---

3. http://www.raspbmc.com/wiki/user/windows-installation/
4. http://svn.stmlabs.com/svn/raspbmc/release/installers/python/install.py

```
⇒ Enter your choice here (e.g. 'disk1', 'disk2'):  disk4
〈 It is your own responsibility to ensure there is no data loss! Please backup
  your system before imaging
  You should also ensure you agree with the Raspbmc License Agreeement
⇒ Are you sure you want to install Raspbmc to '/dev/disk4' and accept the license agreement? [y/N] y
〈 Downloading, please be patient...
  Downloaded 16.35 of 16.35 MiB (100.00%)

  Unmounting all partitions...
  Unmount of all volumes on disk4 was successful
  Please wait while Raspbmc is installed to your SD card...
  This may take some time and no progress will be reported until it has finished.
  0+1172 records in
  0+1172 records out
  76800000 bytes transferred in 6.781433 secs (11325040 bytes/sec)
  Installation complete.
  Would you like to setup your post-installation settings [ADVANCED]? [y/N] N


  Raspbmc is now ready to finish setup on your Pi, please insert the SD card
  with an active internet connection
```

The installation program shows a list of all the drives connected to your PC, including the SD card reader. On your PC the output will be different, but in the previous example, the SD card is mounted under the name disk4. Enter its name and confirm that you'd like to install Raspbmc. Make sure you choose the correct drive, because the installer deletes all the data on the device you've selected!

After you've created a bootable SD card, insert it into the Pi and turn it on. Surprisingly, the Pi won't start XBMC right away; rather, it boots a minimalist Linux system and starts the actual installation of Raspbmc. First it repartitions the SD card and formats the newly created partitions. Then it downloads and installs the root file system, the kernel, some kernel modules, and a few libraries. After a reboot, it eventually downloads and installs the latest version of XBMC.

None of these steps requires user interaction. Depending on the speed of your SD card and your Internet connection, they take about twenty to thirty minutes. So, you can safely go for a walk or have a cup of your favorite hot beverage.

Start Raspbmc for the First Time

After the installation process has finished, Raspbmc starts XBMC automatically. Its main menu looks like Figure 35, *Raspbmc main menu*, on page 78.

At first sight, XBMC looks like many other media players. It has menu items for viewing photos, watching videos, playing music, and configuring some

Figure 35—Raspbmc main menu

system preferences. These functions are mainly self-explanatory—for playing or viewing any kind of content, you can simply select media files from the SD card or a USB device, and XBMC will output them.

To attach a USB device, such as a hard drive or a USB stick, to the Pi, you have to use a USB hub, or you have to temporarily disconnect your mouse and control XBMC using your keyboard. Instead of choosing a menu item by clicking it with the mouse, you can move the focus with the cursor keys and press Return to select an item. When you press the Esc key, you go back one step in the menu hierarchy.

To get the most out of XBMC, you should connect it to your network. If you've connected your Pi using Ethernet, you don't have to do anything; XBMC will recognize it automatically. If you want to use Wi-Fi, choose the Programs > Raspbmc Settings menu. In the Network Configuration tab (see Figure 36, *You can change many settings using the Raspbmc Settings menu*, on page 79), set the Network Mode to Wireless (WIFI) Network. Then enter your wireless network's SSID and your password. Usually, it's beneficial (but not necessary) to set a static IP address for your Pi when it's running XBMC. So disable the Use DHCP button and enter a unique IP address in "IP address." Click the OK button, and you're finished.

XBMC is more than a simple media player; you can improve and enhance it using many add-ons that are available for free on the Web. Simply put,

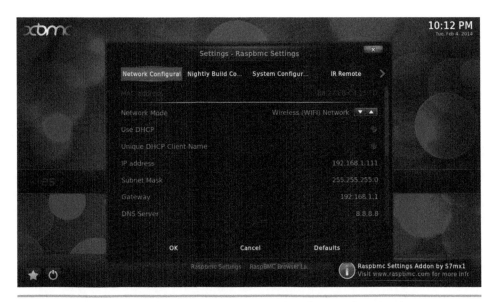

Figure 36—You can change many settings using the Raspbmc Settings menu.

add-ons give you access to media on the Web. For example, you can find add-ons that aggregate the content of certain TV stations or add-ons that give you access to the music of the greatest video games. XBMC even provides a very convenient way to manage add-ons. In Figure 37, *Managing add-ons in XBMC*, on page 80, you can see the TED add-on, which lists the latest and greatest TED conference videos.

Take a few minutes and browse the list of add-ons to see whether there's something interesting to you. When in doubt, install it and take a look. It's easy to remove an add-on if you don't like it. Note that you need to make sure you have enough bandwidth for most add-ons, because they stream a lot of data.

Depending on the speed of your SD card and your Internet connection, you'll experience a noticeable lag when choosing menu items in XBMC. This might get better in future releases, but for the moment you have to live with it and be patient when navigating through XBMC's menus. However, playing content works fine, without any lags or staggering.

Finally, you should take a look at the Systems > Settings menu and see whether all settings match your local setup. If you're using composite video, for example, you have to choose analog as your audio output device in Systems > Settings > Audio.

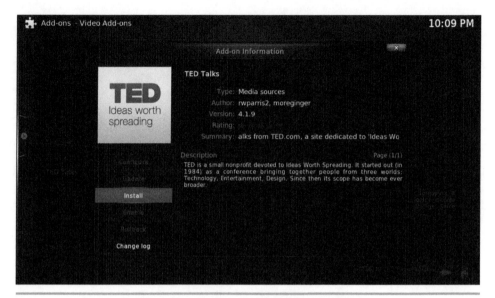

Figure 37—Managing add-ons in XBMC

Add Files to XBMC

In XBMC you can easily add new movies, TV shows, or music using the Add Files menu in the Videos or Music menu. Before you start to add your media files, you should know how XBMC works internally. XBMC is more than a simple media player; it's a full-blown media library that tries to automatically get as much information about your media files as possible. For example, XBMC reads additional information about your favorite TV shows from web databases and adds them to your library. This can be anything from an episode's original air date to a short summary.

To do this, XBMC depends on a certain file-naming scheme—you can read all about it on the project's wiki.[5] Note that choosing the correct filenames and directory structures even affects XBMC's main menu. If you add a directory for TV shows, for example, XBMC adds a TV shows menu item to its main menu. So, to get the most out of XBMC, you should rename your media files accordingly before you import them.

The easiest way to add files to XBMC is to attach a USB device containing your media files directly to the Pi. This solution works fine, but it also has some disadvantages. The USB device often is bigger than the Pi itself, and it

---

5.   http://wiki.xbmc.org/index.php?title=Adding_videos_to_the_library/Naming_files

Video and Music Formats

XBMC supports nearly all container formats and codecs on the market. You'll rarely find a multimedia file that the Pi can't play. There's one problem, though: the Raspberry Foundation licensed hardware acceleration only for the H.264 video codec. Fortunately, this is one of the most popular codecs available, but if you have video files using a different codec, you might not be able to watch them unless you buy a license for them. At the moment, you can buy licenses for MPEG-2 and VC-1 online.[a] You provide your Pi's serial number and get back a license key that you enter in Raspbmc's Settings menu.

a. http://www.raspberrypi.com/license-keys/

probably consumes more power, too. In addition, it requires at least one of your valuable USB ports. A better solution is to store media on the SD card or to stream media from your local network. Because of XBMC's great network integration, you can implement both solutions easily.

XBMC supports FTP, SFTP, SSH, NFS, and Samba out of the box, and you don't have to configure much to get them all up and running. XBMC enables SSH by default, so to copy data to the SD card, you can use scp, for example, as you did in *Use Secure Shell with the Pi*, on page 56. Run the following command from your PC's terminal to create a folder named Movies in XBMC's home directory:

```
maik> ssh pi@192.168.2.109 "mkdir /home/pi/Movies"
```

Replace the IP address with your Pi's address. Note that Raspbmc also comes with a user named pi that has the password raspberry at the moment. Now you can copy media files using scp and add them to the XBMC library afterward.

```
maik> scp Pulp\ Fiction\ (1994).avi pi@192.168.2.109:Movies
```

Even if you use an SD card with plenty of space, it probably won't be enough to store your whole media library. Also, it doesn't make sense to always copy files before you can watch a film or listen to some music. That's what network file systems such as NFS and Samba were built for, and XBMC supports them all.

Using NFS or Samba, you can host all your media files on your regular PC and stream them to the Pi when you want to use them. Configuring NFS[6] or

---

6. http://wiki.xbmc.org/index.php?title=NFS

Samba[7] is beyond the scope of this book, but the XBMC wiki has excellent documentation for all major platforms.

As soon as your media files are available in your home network via NFS or Samba, you can easily access them using XBMC. For NFS you don't usually have to do anything, and you can configure your Samba settings in the System > Service > SMB client menu.

Control XBMC Remotely

If you want to use the Pi as a multimedia center in your living room, sooner or later you'll want a remote control. If you have a modern TV, chances are good that you can control the Pi using your TV's remote control. Modern TV sets use the HDMI cable not only for transferring video and audio data, but also for transmitting remote-control commands. In this case, your TV set will send remote-control commands automatically to the Raspberry Pi.

If your TV isn't quite as modern, you can use some special hardware with an infrared dongle,[8] but the easiest method is just to use your smartphone.

Not only does XBMC have add-ons for managing your multimedia files, it also allows you to install web interfaces for controlling XBMC remotely. Go to the System > Settings > Services > Webserver menu and enable the "Allow control of XBMC via HTTP" option. Then click the "Web interface" button and select Get More. In Figure 38, *XBMC comes with several web interfaces*, on page 83, you can see the currently available web interfaces. Enable all of them so you can try them and choose your favorite.

After you've enabled the web interface, you can use it with every browser that has access to your network. The interface listens on port 80, so in your browser, you only have to enter your Pi's IP address, such as http://192.168.2.109, to open XBMC's web interface. (Remember to replace the IP address with your Pi's IP address.) In Figure 39, *The AWXi web interface in action*, on page 83, you can see the AWXi web interface in action, for example. It has all the usual buttons, such as play, pause, and stop, and it allows you to search your whole media library.

If you have an iPad/iPhone[9] or an Android phone,[10] you can even install a native remote control application for XBMC. In Figure 40, *Control XBMC on*

---

7. http://wiki.xbmc.org/index.php?title=Samba
8. http://www.raspbmc.com/wiki/user/configuring-remotes/
9. http://itunes.apple.com/gb/app/official-xbmc-remote/id520480364
10. https://play.google.com/store/apps/details?id=org.xbmc.android.remote

Figure 38—XBMC comes with several web interfaces.

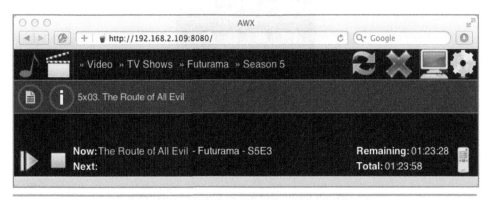

Figure 39—The AWXi web interface in action

an Android device, on page 84 and Figure 41, *It looks and works like a regular remote*, on page 84, you can see the Android version. It not only looks beautiful, but it also provides convenient access to all XBMC functions. In many regards, it's much better than a regular TV remote.

If you're still not satisfied with the remote control, you can search for even more advanced XBMC remote control apps. At the time of this writing, one is Yatse,[11] and more will probably be available soon.

---

11. https://play.google.com/store/apps/details?id=org.leetzone.android.yatsewidgetfree

Figure 40—Control XBMC on an Android device.

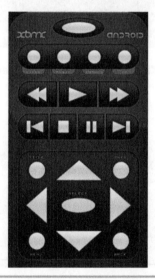

Figure 41—It looks and works like a regular remote.

Next Steps

In this chapter, you learned to do something completely different with the Pi. For the first time, you didn't use it as a regular PC; instead, you turned it into a special-purpose device, a multimedia center. In the next chapter, you'll learn how to run even more multimedia applications on your Pi, and you'll play some entertaining games.

CHAPTER 8

Play Games on Your Pi

Linux has never been a popular gaming platform. Even though the situation has improved over the years, it probably will take some time for the first blockbuster titles to become available. Still, you can already play some entertaining and sometimes even addictive games on the Raspberry Pi.

For example, you can enjoy thousands of text adventure games on the Pi. Although commercial publishers abandoned this genre long ago, it still has an active and enthusiastic fan base that releases new games frequently. And if you haven't played classic games such as *Zork*, you should give them a try.

Another classic genre is point-and-click adventure, including games such as *The Secret of Monkey Island* and *Day of the Tentacle*. Thanks to the efforts of the open-source community, you can play most titles on your Pi.

Even if the Pi isn't powerful enough to run modern games, it still has enough power to run some native Linux games, such as *Quake III*. It even has enough power to emulate some home computers and game consoles from the past. For example, on the Pi you can play all games made for Atari's VCS 2600.

Play Interactive Fiction

Text adventure games were very popular with users of the first home computers. In contrast to modern games with spectacular 3D graphics and surround sound, text adventures look very spartan. They output only text, and you control the game by typing commands on your keyboard. Here you can see the opening of *Zork*, one of the most famous text adventures.

```
ZORK I: The Great Underground Empire
Copyright (c) 1981, 1982, 1983 Infocom, Inc. All rights reserved.
ZORK is a registered trademark of Infocom, Inc.
Revision 88 / Serial number 840726
West of House
```

```
You are standing in an open field west of a white house, with a
boarded front door.
There is a small mailbox here.
```

⇒ **>open mailbox**
❮ Opening the small mailbox reveals a leaflet.

⇒ **>take leaflet**
❮ Taken.

⇒ **>read leaflet**
❮ "WELCOME TO ZORK!

```
ZORK is a game of adventure, danger, and low cunning. In it you will
explore some of the most amazing territory
ever seen by mortals. No computer should be without one!"
```

Don't be misled by the game's presentation. Many text adventures tell great stories and can entertain you for hours.

Even though no commercial text adventures have been released for decades, the genre still has an active community that produces exciting games. Most of these games tell long and elaborate stories, so their authors prefer to call their creations *interactive fiction*.

Infocom was one of the first companies to produce interactive fiction. They created some of the greatest text adventure games. The Infocom developers realized early on that they could reduce their efforts by creating a domain-specific language for describing interactive fiction. They called this language *Z-language*, and authors of interactive fiction still use it today to create games.

To run programs written in Z-language, you need an implementation of a virtual machine named Z-machine,[1] and one of the best is Frotz.[2] You can install it as follows:

pi@raspberrypi ~ $ **sudo apt-get install frotz**

To play a text adventure using Frotz, you need only the game's Z-language file. A great place to start your search for interactive fiction is the Interactive Fiction Archive,[3] which hosts thousands of games.

If you're new to interactive fiction, you should start your journey with the *Zork* trilogy. This series of games made Infocom famous, and although they are a couple of decades old, they are still as fresh as they were on their first

---

1. http://en.wikipedia.org/wiki/Z-machine
2. http://frotz.sourceforge.net/
3. http://www.ifarchive.org/

day. Meanwhile, they are available for free,[4] so download *Zork I* [5] and start it as follows:

```
pi@raspberrypi ~ $ unzip zork1.zip
pi@raspberrypi ~ $ frotz zork1/DATA/ZORK1.DAT
```

This invokes the Z-machine interpreter and runs the game stored in ZORK1.DAT. You might need a few moments to get used to this kind of game,[6] but it's certainly well worth it.

If you enjoy playing interactive fiction, you might also enjoy creating it using today's tools. It's really easy,[7] at least on a technical level. You still have to come up with a compelling and original story, though.

Play Point-and-Click Adventures

Another genre that has always been popular is point-and-click adventures. In these games, you control the main character using the mouse. You can make the character move to a certain place on the screen by clicking the place, and you can perform actions by clicking the action's name on the screen. Popular point-and-click adventures are *The Secret of Monkey Island*, *Day of the Tentacle*, and *Maniac Mansion*.

There has always been a demand for new point-and-click adventures, but very few have been released over the last several years. The big publishers didn't believe in them and preferred to release countless first-person shooters, such as *Call of Duty* and *Battlefield*, instead.

Tim Schafer, one of the creators of *The Secret of Monkey Island*, got frustrated by this situation and tried to raise some money on Kickstarter.com to fund a new point-and-click adventure. He raised more than $3.3 million and proved that people are still very interested in this genre.

Similar to text adventures, most point-and-click adventures run on a virtual machine. The most popular one is SCUMM, which stands for Script Creation Utility for Maniac Mansion.

Originally, it was created by the developers of LucasArts to implement the game *Maniac Mansion*, and they have used it to implement many other games since.

---

4. http://www.infocom-if.org/downloads/downloads.html
5. http://www.infocom-if.org/downloads/zork1.zip
6. At http://pr-if.org/doc/play-if-card/play-if-card.html, you can find a nice help sheet.
7. http://inform7.com/

The ScummVM[8] project implements a virtual machine that interprets SCUMM games, and it's available for free. You can install it as follows:

```
pi@raspberrypi ~ $ sudo apt-get install scummvm
pi@raspberrypi ~ $ sudo apt-get install beneath-a-steel-sky
pi@raspberrypi ~ $ sudo apt-get install flight-of-the-amazon-queen
```

This will install not only ScummVM, but also two great games you can play with it. These games will appear in the Games section of your desktop's Start menu. In the following figure, you can see *Beneath a Steel Sky*.

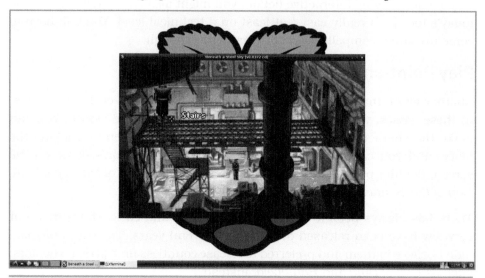

Figure 42—*Beneath a Steel Sky* is still a great game.

Beneath a Steel Sky and *Flight of the Amazon Queen* are freeware, so you can safely install them. Most other games aren't available for free, so you're allowed to install them only if you own the original. If you own other games that are compatible with ScummVM, you can start ScummVM directly and add them.

Emulate Other Platforms

Another way to play some fine games on the Pi is to emulate other platforms. Many emulators are available for Linux, and they reanimate classic computers and game consoles, such as the Commodore 64, the Sega Mega Drive, the Nintendo Entertainment System (NES), and many more. There's probably at least one emulator for every single system from the past.

---

8.   http://www.scummvm.org/

An emulator rebuilds the hardware of a certain computer or game console in software. So, you run the emulator on the Pi, and then you can work with the emulated system as if you're using the original hardware. Most importantly, you can run all the old software and games that were available for the old system.

Emulating a complete computer is extremely difficult even for simple systems, and most emulators suffer from two major problems. The first is accuracy; often an emulator can't emulate the original system at 100 percent. The second problem is performance, because emulating even very old and slow hardware requires a tremendous amount of resources. For example, the Commodore 64 ran at a clock speed of only 1MHz, but you need a lot of computing power to emulate it. Even the Pi's hardware isn't powerful enough to emulate the C64 at a reasonable frame rate at the moment, although it has a multiple of the C64's resources. This might change with better graphics drivers for the Pi.

Still, the Pi is powerful enough to emulate some cool game consoles, and one of them is the Atari VCS 2600.[9] This device was popular from 1977 until the early 1990s, and you could play great games such as *Pac-Man*, *Centipede*, and *Pitfall* on it. The console was so popular that several emulators exist for it, and one of the best is Stella.[10] You can install and start it as follows:

```
pi@raspberrypi ~ $ sudo apt-get install stella
pi@raspberrypi ~ $ stella
```

First Stella asks you where it should look for game ROMs. The games for the VCS 2600 shipped on cartridges containing a few kilobytes of read-only memory (ROM). To play a game using Stella, you need a copy of its cartridge's ROM. You can copy the content of a cartridge to your PC using a special device. Fortunately, you can find ROM files for all games on the Web,[11] but there's one big problem: although most games for the VCS 2600 are very old, they are still copyrighted. So in most countries, it's illegal to download and use ROM files of games you don't actually own!

You can buy used cartridges on the Web for very little money, and some publishers still sell Atari game collections that ship on CDs. These collections do nothing but run an emulator and play the original ROM files.

---

9. http://en.wikipedia.org/wiki/Atari_2600
10. http://stella.sourceforge.net/
11. http://atariage.com/

The size of a ROM file is usually between 4KB and 8KB, and the filenames end with the extension .bin. So, *Pac-Man*'s ROM file is named pacman.bin, for example. If you've copied a ROM file to the Pi, you can select it in Stella's main menu, and it will start immediately. By default, you can use the cursor keys for movements and the spacebar for actions. Stella allows you to remap all keys, and it also has support for joysticks. On top of that, you can change countless video and audio options, but note that the Pi won't emulate the VCS 2600 properly in the most demanding video modes.

Playing some classic games might bring back childhood memories, but the VCS 2600 has an incredibly active user group that still creates games.[12] Many of these home-brew titles actually look and sound better than most of the original games, and they're usually available for free. In the following figure, you can see *A-VCS-tec Challenge*, for example.[13] Some of these home-brew games are available on cartridges even today.

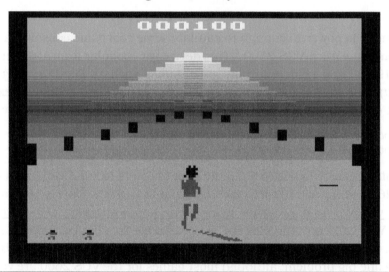

Figure 43—People still create great games for the VCS 2600.

By the way, developing games or demos for the VCS 2600 is very difficult, but you can learn a lot, and it can be fun! Most people can't imagine how limited the hardware was. It ran at a clock speed of 1.19MHz, it had only 128 bytes of RAM, and it had no frame buffer for the video display. Developing software for this machine was really painful back in the old days, but today's tools and documentation make it much easier. For example, Stella comes

---

12. http://en.wikipedia.org/wiki/Atari_2600_homebrew

13. http://www.quernhorst.de/atari/ac.html

with a debugger that allows you to see and change the state of a game while it's running. To enable the debugger, start Stella like this:

```
pi@raspberrypi ~ $ stella -debug
```

To invoke the debugger, press the backquote key (`), and remember that you can freely remap Stella's actions to other keys if you can't find them on your keyboard. In the following figure, you can see the debugger in action.

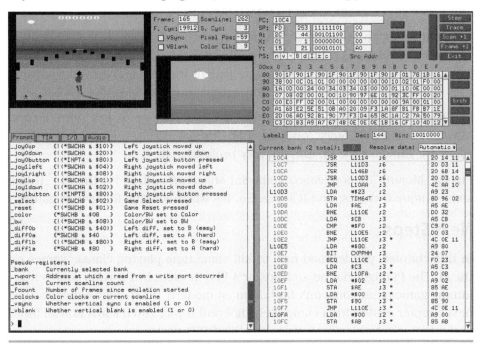

Figure 44—Stella comes with a powerful debugger.

All in all, Stella works pretty well on the Pi, because the VCS 2600 isn't a very strong machine. Emulators for other systems don't work as well at the moment. The C64 emulator Vice,[14] for example, theoretically works on the Pi, but its frame rate is too low for playing most games. On the other hand, emulators such as MAME[15] work really well for many titles.

Play Native Games

In the preceding sections, you learned about technologies that help you run games using virtual machines and emulators, but native games also exist for

---

14. http://vice-emu.sourceforge.net/
15. http://mamedev.org/

Linux. For example, on the LXDE desktop, you can find a compilation of some classic games written in Python: *Four in a Row*, *Snake*, and so on.

Because the Pi is a regular Linux system, you can run every game compatible with your current distribution as long as the Pi's resources are sufficient. If you search the Web for classic games, such as *Tetris* or *Pac-Man*, you'll quickly find really good clones.

```
pi@raspberrypi ~ $ sudo apt-get install ltris pacman
```

It's worth trying to install all the games you find, but many are too demanding for the Pi. Surprisingly, the Pi is capable of running *Quake II* and *Quake III* (two famous first-person shooters) at a decent frame rate. As of this writing, they have some problems with sound output, but they're still playable.

In addition, you can find cool games in the Pi Store (see *Install Software and Media Using the Pi Store*, on page 38). *Iridium Rising*, for example, is an exclusive game for the Pi, and it's very professional.

Finally, Mojang[16] has released a special *Minecraft* edition for the Pi.[17] It has some unique features, and it's free. So, it's worth looking for new Pi games.

Next Steps

In this chapter, you learned how to kill some time playing classic games on the Pi. The Pi might not be an Xbox or a PlayStation, but it runs some entertaining games that you won't find on most modern video game consoles. The next chapter deals with a completely different topic. You'll learn how to build and attach electronics projects to the Pi's GPIO ports.

---

16. http://www.mojang.com/
17. http://www.raspberrypi.org/archives/3263

CHAPTER 9

Tinker with the GPIO Pins

The Raspberry Foundation built the Pi not only to teach kids how to program, but also to teach them how to tinker with electronics. That's why the Pi has an expansion header that makes it easy to connect it to your own electronics projects.

In this chapter, you'll learn how to build your own small electronics devices and control them with the Pi. We'll start slowly and build a very basic circuit that makes a light-emitting diode (LED) shine. After that, we'll control the LED using the Pi's expansion header, and we'll turn the LED on and off by issuing commands from the Pi.

Then we'll build a small memory alarm that shows how much memory is left on the Pi. It will work like a traffic light, where a red light indicates that the amount of remaining memory is critically low. In addition, we'll make the results of the memory alarm available in a web browser.

What You Need

To build all projects in this chapter, you need only a few cheap parts. (You can see them all in Figure 45, *The parts you need*, on page 94.)

- A half-size breadboard

- Three 5mm LEDs (red, yellow, and green)

- Three resistors in the range of 220Ω to 1kΩ

- Four female/male jumper wires

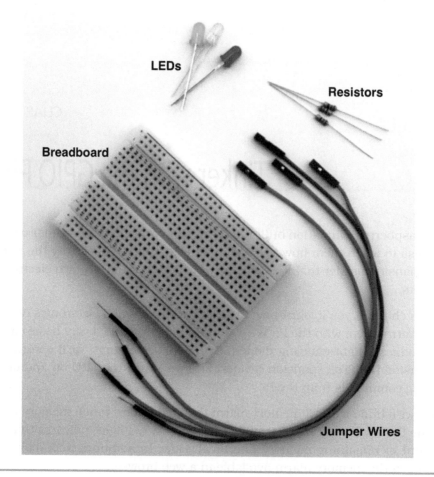

Figure 45—The parts you need

You can get these parts at any shop that sells electronic parts—for example, RadioShack,[1] SparkFun,[2] Mouser,[3] Digi-Key,[4] and Adafruit.[5] Note that buying single LEDs, resistors, or jumper wires doesn't make much sense. You can get these parts for much cheaper when you buy them as a pack. For example, RadioShack sells packs of LEDs (catalog number 276-1622) and resistors (catalog number 271-308). Adafruit has a nice pack of jumper wires (product ID 826), and it also sells breadboards (product ID 64).

---

1. http://radioshack.com
2. http://www.sparkfun.com/
3. http://mouser.com
4. http://digikey.com
5. http://adafruit.com

Meet the Pi's GPIO Pins

To connect your own electronics projects to the Pi, you can use the expansion header in the top-left corner of the Pi (see Figure 1, *The front side of a Model B (Revision 1)*, on page 2). It consists of twenty-six pins arranged in two rows containing thirteen pins each. The top row contains the even-numbered pins, and the other row contains the odd-numbered pins. That is, the first pin in the lower row is pin 1, and you can find the label "P1" on the Pi below the pin.

In the following figure, you can see the meaning and the numbering of the pins. Note that the meaning of some pins has changed between revision 1 and revision 2. With the pins labeled Ground, the Pi can share a common ground with our electronics projects. Using the pins labeled 3v3 and 5V, you can power external devices connected to the Pi with 3.3 volts or 5 volts. The Pi limits the output of pin 1 to 50mA, while pin 2 allows for a current draw that depends on the USB input current. If you power the Pi with a 1A power supply, for example, you can draw up to 300mA from pin 2, because the Pi Model B needs 700mA for itself.

Rev 2	5V	5V	Ground	GPIO14	GPIO15	GPIO18	Ground	GPIO23	GPIO24	Ground	GPIO25	GPIO8	GPIO7
Rev 1	5V	-	Ground	GPIO14	GPIO15	GPIO18	-	GPIO23	GPIO24	-	GPIO25	GPIO8	GPIO7
	↑	↑	↑	↑	↑	↑	↑	↑	↑	↑	↑	↑	↑
Pin	2	4	6	8	10	12	14	16	18	20	22	24	26
Pin	1	3	5	7	9	11	13	15	17	19	21	23	25
	↓	↓	↓	↓	↓	↓	↓	↓	↓	↓	↓	↓	↓
Rev 1	3v3	GPIO0	GPIO1	GPIO4	-	GPIO17	GPIO21	GPIO22	-	GPIO10	GPIO9	GPIO11	-
Rev 2	3v3	GPIO2	GPIO3	GPIO4	Ground	GPIO17	GPIO27	GPIO22	3v3	GPIO10	GPIO9	GPIO11	Ground

Figure 46—The Pi's GPIO pins

In revision 1, pins 4, 9, 14, 17, 20, and 25 were reserved for future enhancements, so you couldn't use them in your own projects. The remaining pins are general-purpose input/output (GPIO) pins that you can use as digital input or output pins. Note that the GPIO pin names don't correspond to the pin numbers of the expansion header.

You can use the GPIO pins, for example, to read the state of a push button or to turn an LED on and off. For this chapter's examples, you can assume that all GPIO pins work the same, but you should know that some of the Pi's pins are special. Pin 12, for example, supports pulse-width modulation (PWM),[6]

6.   http://en.wikipedia.org/wiki/Pulse_width_modulation

which can be handy for controlling motors. If you're going to build more complex projects, you should take a look at a more detailed description of the Pi's pins.[7]

Build a Basic Circuit

To warm up, we'll build one of the most basic circuits possible. We'll connect an LED to the Pi and make it shine as long as the Pi is running. For this we'll need an LED, a resistor, a breadboard, and two female/male jumper wires. Using these parts, we'll build the circuit shown in the following figure.

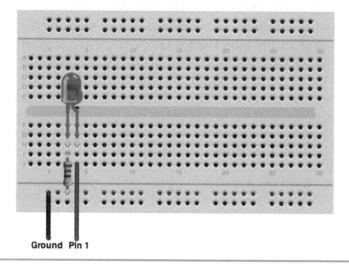

Ground Pin 1

Figure 47—A basic circuit

Before we actually build the circuit, you should know what all the parts are for and how they work. Breadboards are useful tools for prototyping circuits. You can simply plug in parts such as LEDs and resistors, and you don't have to solder them. Breadboards come in various sizes, but they all look very similar. On all of them, you can find many sockets arranged in columns. Most breadboards also have two rows of sockets at the top and at the bottom.

The main trick of a breadboard is that it automatically connects the sockets belonging to a certain column and to a certain row. In the basic circuit shown in the preceding figure, you connect the Pi's ground pin to the second-to-last row of the breadboard. This automatically connects all sockets in this row to the Pi's ground (which is why all the sockets in this row are light green). The same happens in the two columns connected to the LED. The resistor indirectly

7.   http://elinux.org/RPi_Low-level_peripherals

connects the Pi's ground pin to one of the LED's connectors. In addition, you connect the Pi's pin 1 directly to the other connector of the LED by plugging it into a socket in the same column.

By the way, LED stands for light-emitting diode, so an LED is basically a diode. Diodes are useful because they let electricity pass in only one direction. That's true for LEDs, too, and LEDs emit light as a side effect.

Working with LEDs isn't very difficult, but we have to take care of a few things. First, we have to connect them the right way. LEDs have two wires, and one of them is a bit shorter than the other. The shorter wire is called a *cathode* (negative), and we have to connect it to the Pi's ground pin. The longer wire is called an *anode* (positive), and we have to connect it to one of the Pi's power supply or GPIO pins. You can also identify the anode and cathode by taking a close look at the LED's case. The flat side belongs to the cathode and the round side to the anode. In Figure 47, *A basic circuit*, on page 96, the anode is slightly bent.

Also, you always have to put a resistor in front of an LED. If you don't, the LED will consume too much power and will be destroyed. Simply put, a resistor limits the amount of current that flows through an electric connection and protects the LED. Calculating the resistor value for a certain type of LED isn't difficult, but it's beyond the scope of this book. Simply keep in mind that the lower the resistor value, the brighter the light will shine. When in doubt, use a 330Ω or 470Ω resistor.

Now it's time to actually build the circuit. First, connect the LED to the breadboard. Make sure that the LED's direction is correct, and plug it in. You have to press firmly but not too hard—otherwise, you'll bend the connectors, and they won't fit. It's usually easier to plug in parts after you've shortened the connectors. When cutting the connectors, wear safety glasses to protect your eyes!

The resistor is next, and this time the direction doesn't matter. Before plugging in the resistor, you have to bend its connectors. Also, it usually helps to shorten them.

Finally, connect the two jumper wires to the Pi and to the breadboard. Connect the female side to the Pi and the male side to the breadboard. Make sure you're using the correct pins on the Pi, and then turn on the Pi. If you've connected everything correctly, the LED will turn on, too. Otherwise, take a look at *What If It Doesn't Work?*, on page 105.

Control an LED Using the GPIO Pins

Making an LED shine is a fun exercise, but it gets boring pretty quickly. In this section, you'll learn how to control an LED using software—we'll turn it on and off by issuing commands on the Pi.

Programming hardware directly is usually a difficult task. Using the WiringPi project,[8] it becomes a piece of cake. WiringPi is an open-source project that hides the ugly low-level functions behind a nice, clean interface. If you've worked with the popular Arduino project[9] before, WiringPi will look very familiar because it tries to bring most of the Arduino goodies to the Pi. WiringPi not only makes programming the Pi's hardware easier, but it also comes with a small command-line utility named gpio that allows you to control the hardware without writing code.

You can install WiringPi on the Pi as follows:

```
pi@raspberry:~$ cd /tmp
pi@raspberry:~$ sudo apt-get install git-core
pi@raspberry:~$ sudo apt-get update
pi@raspberry:~$ sudo apt-get upgrade
pi@raspberry:~$ git clone git://git.drogon.net/wiringPi
pi@raspberry:~$ cd wiringPi
pi@raspberry:~$ ./build
```

These commands install the WiringPi libraries and the gpio command. You can use WiringPi from many programming languages, such as C, C++, Python, Ruby, and so on. In this chapter, we'll use it exclusively from the command line and in a short but effective shell script.

All we need for our first interactive electronics experiments is the gpio command. It supports many useful options and a lot of powerful commands. The most important ones are mode, read, and write. For example, the following command sets the GPIO18 pin into output mode:

```
pi@raspberry:~$ gpio -g mode 18 out
```

All GPIO pins can be in one of the following modes in, out, pwm, up, down, or tri. We're only interested in in and out at the moment. To read digital signals from a GPIO pin, set its mode to in. Set it to out if you'd like to emit digital signals. You have to set a pin's mode only once, and the pin will remember its mode until you set it to a different one.

---

8. http://wiringpi.com/
9. http://arduino.cc

After you've set GPIO18's mode to out, you can turn it on like this:

```
pi@raspberry:~$ gpio -g write 18 1
```

Turning it off works similarly:

```
pi@raspberry:~$ gpio -g write 18 0
```

Finally, you can read GPIO18's current state using the read command:

```
pi@raspberry:~$ gpio -g read 18
0
```

This command returns 0 if there's currently no signal and 1 otherwise.

With gpio, we can control the LED on our breadboard easily. You have to connect it to only one of the Pi's GPIO pins instead of connecting it directly to a power-supply pin. For example, you can use GPIO18, which is pin 12 in Figure 46, *The Pi's GPIO pins*, on page 95. Choosing and addressing the correct pins can be a bit confusing because of the different naming and numbering schemes. By default, WiringPi uses its own numbering scheme,[10] but for our first experiments we'll use the official GPIO pin names. Fortunately, gpio accepts them when you pass it the -g option.

So, in the circuit, disconnect the jumper wire from pin 1 and connect it to pin 12 instead. Then run the following commands:

```
pi@raspberry:~$ gpio -g mode 18 out
pi@raspberry:~$ gpio -g write 18 1
```

These commands will turn on the LED, and the following command will turn it off:

```
pi@raspberry:~$ gpio -g write 18 0
```

gpio supports many more commands and options, and it really pays to read its manual page. For example, with the readall command, you can look at the current state of all the Pi's GPIO pins (see Figure 48, *Results of the readall command*, on page 100).

With only a few parts and a single command-line tool, we've created our first circuit. Even better, we can control it with the Raspberry Pi! In the next section, we'll create a more complex project using the techniques we've discussed so far.

---

10. https://projects.drogon.net/raspberry-pi/wiringpi/pins/

```
pi@raspberry:~$ gpio readall
+----------+------+--------+-------+
| wiringPi | GPIO | Name   | Value |
+----------+------+--------+-------+
|        0 |   17 | GPIO 0 | Low   |
|        1 |   18 | GPIO 1 | Low   |
|        2 |   27 | GPIO 2 | Low   |
|        3 |   22 | GPIO 3 | Low   |
|        4 |   23 | GPIO 4 | Low   |
|        5 |   24 | GPIO 5 | Low   |
|        6 |   25 | GPIO 6 | Low   |
|        7 |    4 | GPIO 7 | Low   |
|        8 |    2 | SDA    | High  |
|        9 |    3 | SCL    | High  |
|       10 |    8 | CE0    | Low   |
|       11 |    7 | CE1    | Low   |
|       12 |   10 | MOSI   | Low   |
|       13 |    9 | MISO   | Low   |
|       14 |   11 | SCLK   | Low   |
|       15 |   14 | TxD    | High  |
|       16 |   15 | RxD    | High  |
+----------+------+--------+-------+
|       17 |   28 | GPIO 8 | Low   |
|       18 |   29 | GPIO 9 | Low   |
|       19 |   30 | GPIO10 | Low   |
|       20 |   31 | GPIO11 | Low   |
+----------+------+--------+-------+
```

Figure 48—Results of the readall command

Build an Out-of-Memory Alarm

Turning an LED on and off using software is an important exercise, but it's certainly not a very useful project. Usually, you won't control LEDs manually, but you'll use them as status indicators. For example, many USB devices use LEDs to show whether they're reading or writing data at the moment.

In this section, we'll use three LEDs as status indicators for the Pi's current memory usage. The LEDs will have the same colors as a traffic light. If the Pi's memory is critically low, we'll turn on the red light. If a lot of memory is available, we'll turn on the green light. Otherwise, it will be yellow.

In Figure 49, *Memory alarm circuit diagram*, on page 101, you can see the circuit of the memory alarm. In Figure 50, *The memory alarm circuit*, on page 101, you can see it in real life. It's very similar to the last circuit we built. We have to copy the original LED circuit only two times to control three LEDs.

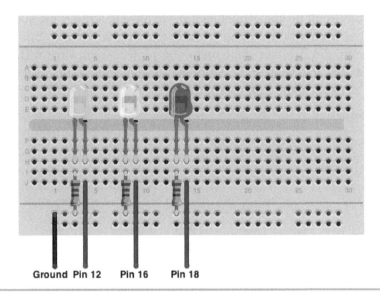

Ground Pin 12   Pin 16   Pin 18

Figure 49—Memory alarm circuit diagram

Figure 50—The memory alarm circuit

To make the circuit do something useful, we have to write some software. We could choose from a broad range of programming languages, but thanks to the gpio command, we can implement the project's software with a simple shell script. The following statements define some constants and functions. Also, they perform some initializations.

gpio/memwatch.sh

```
Line 1  #!/bin/bash
     -  green=18
     -  yellow=23
     -  red=24
     5
     -  init_leds()
     -  {
     -    for i in $green $yellow $red
     -    do
    10      gpio -g mode $i out
     -      gpio -g write $i 0
     -    done
     -  }
     -
    15  set_led()
     -  {
     -    led_status=`gpio -g read $1`
     -    if [ "$led_status" -ne 1 ]
     -    then
    20      init_leds
     -      gpio -g write $1 1
     -    fi
     -  }
     -
    25  cleanup()
     -  {
     -    init_leds
     -    exit 0
     -  }
    30
     -  init_leds
     -  trap cleanup INT TERM EXIT
```

The first three lines define constants for the GPIO pins to which we've connected the LEDs. Note that the numbers in the constants refer to the pin names GPIO18, GPIO23, and GPIO24. They don't refer to the expansion header's pin numbers 12, 16, and 18.

The init_leds() function in line 6 sets the mode of all three LEDs to output and turns them off. The set_led() function turns on a certain LED and turns off the other ones. Before turning on the LED, it checks whether the LED is already on. This ensures that the LED doesn't flicker in case the current status hasn't changed. Finally, the cleanup() function turns off all LEDs and exits the program.

To initialize the program, we have to call init_leds(). To make sure that the program cleans up before it stops, we can use the trap command in line 32. This command binds the cleanup() method to the most common exit signals, so if we terminate the script, it will call cleanup() before it shuts down.

Now that we've initialized everything properly, we can write the alarm's business logic. Therefore, we need to find a way to determine the Pi's current memory status, and the free command is the perfect solution to this problem.

```
pi@raspberry:~$ free
              total      used       free     shared    buffers     cached
Mem:         190836     40232     150604          0       6252      21068
-/+ buffers/cache:      12912     177924
Swap:             0          0          0
```

To calculate the percentage of memory available, we have to cut out the amount of total memory and the amount of free memory from the free command's output. After that, we have to turn on the correct LED depending on the percentage value. Here's how to do this:

gpio/memwatch.sh
```
Line 1  while :
     -  do
     -    total=`free | grep Mem | tr -s ' ' | cut -d ' ' -f 2`
     -    free=`free | grep Mem | tr -s ' ' | cut -d ' ' -f 4`
     5    available=$(( free * 100 / total ))
     -    echo -n "$available% of memory available -> "
     -
     -    if [ "$available" -le 10 ]
     -    then
    10      echo "Critical"
     -      set_led $red
     -    elif [ "$available" -le 30 ]
     -    then
     -      echo "Low"
    15      set_led $yellow
     -    else
     -      echo "OK"
     -      set_led $green
     -    fi
    20    sleep 10
     -  done
```

The memory monitor should permanently check the current memory status so the whole logic runs in an endless loop. Lines 3 to 5 calculate the percentage of memory available by calling the free command two times and cutting out the relevant information. Note that this solution has a potential flaw. If the current memory usage changes significantly between the two calls to free, we'll get bad results. This isn't very likely, but it might happen, so for a production system we'd have to find a more sophisticated way to determine the current memory usage. For a prototype, it's sufficient.

The following lines compare the memory available to a few threshold values. If the available memory is less than or equal to 10 percent of the total memory, the program turns on the red LED. If it's between 10 and 30 percent, it turns on the yellow LED. Otherwise, the green LED will shine. Finally, the program goes to sleep for 10 seconds, so it doesn't waste a lot of CPU time.

Now type in the shell script or download it by clicking the filename above the code, and copy it to the Pi. The following statement will make the script executable:

```
pi@raspberry:~$ chmod a+x memwatch.sh
```

Then you can start it as follows:

```
pi@raspberry:~$ ./memwatch.sh
78% of memory available -> OK
```

To test the out-of-memory alarm, start the LXDE desktop environment and run the script in a terminal. Then open a few applications and see how the amount of available memory shrinks.

Display the GPIO Status in a Browser

In Chapter 6, *Networking with the Pi*, on page 53, you learned how to set up a web server and PHP5 on the Pi. Now we can use this web server to display the Pi's current memory usage in a web browser. Copy the following PHP program to your Pi's /var/www directory:

gpio/memwatch.php
```php
<?php
    function led_is_on($number) {
        $status = trim(@shell_exec("/usr/local/bin/gpio -g read " . $number));
        if ($status == "0") {
            return False;
        } else {
            return True;
        }
    }
    $green = 18;
    $yellow = 23;
    $red = 24;
    echo "<h1>Memory Usage is ";
```

```
    if (led_is_on($green)) {
        echo "OK";
    }
    elseif (led_is_on($yellow)) {
        echo "Low";
    }
    elseif (led_is_on($red)) {
        echo "Critical";
    }
    else {
        echo "Unknown";
    }
    echo ".</h1>";
?>
```

Start the memwatch.sh script and then point your browser to the memwatch.php file. If the Pi's IP address is 192.168.2.109, for example, we have to use the URL *http://192.168.2.109/memwatch.php*. The browser will display a short message explaining the current memory situation on the Pi.

Even if you've never used PHP before, you should be able to understand what the program does. In the led_is_on() function, it calls the gpio command and reads the current status of a GPIO pin. If the pin is currently on, the function returns True; otherwise, it returns False. After that, the program checks which of the LEDs is on and emits a corresponding message.

As you've seen, it's easy to make the status of an electronics device available in your network. Of course, you can make this page more colorful and turn it into a real traffic-light display, but that is beyond the scope of this book.

What If It Doesn't Work?

Building your own electronics devices isn't rocket science, but it's not extremely simple, either. If you've never worked with a breadboard, LEDs, and resistors before, many things can and will go wrong. Even if you have a lot of experience, you'll still make mistakes.

If something doesn't work as expected, don't panic! Usually, the cause of the problem is very simple. The first thing you should check is whether you've connected all parts to the correct pins. Then you should check the direction of the LEDs. Also, make sure that all parts fit correctly into place. Plugging parts into breadboards can be tricky, especially when the breadboard is new.

Don't forget to plug in the power supply, and don't proceed with your project until you have the simplest version working.

Next Steps

In this chapter, you learned how to build your own electronics projects and control them with the Raspberry Pi. Even though you used only a few cheap parts, you could actually build something fun and useful.

The next chapter will show you how to do even more exciting stuff. You'll connect digital and analog sensors to the Pi, so you can detect motion and measure the current temperature, for example.

CHAPTER 10

Working with Digital and Analog Sensors

Sensors are everywhere today, and many of them have become so ubiquitous that often you don't even notice them. When entering a grocery store, you expect the doors to open automatically. Using temperature sensors, your car automatically turns on the heat to defrost the side mirrors. Distance sensors help you to navigate even the tiniest parking spots.

Of course, you can also find plenty of sensors in your tablet PC and in your smartphone. For example, acceleration sensors turn the screen to landscape or portrait mode automatically; you can also use them for controlling video games.

Attaching sensors to a PC usually isn't so easy. Fortunately, the Pi is different—you can connect it to many intelligent sensors with little effort, although it's still not as easy as using sensors with a microcontroller board, such as the Arduino. In this chapter, you'll learn how to enhance your Pi with both digital and analog sensors.

What You Need

To build all the projects in this chapter, you need the parts you see in Figure 51, *The parts you need*, on page 108.

- A half-size breadboard
- A PIR sensor
- A TMP36 temperature sensor
- An MCP3008-I/P analog-to-digital converter
- Six female/male jumper wires
- Some wires

You already learned where you can get a breadboard and wires in *What You Need*, on page 93. Most of the vendors mentioned there also sell the two

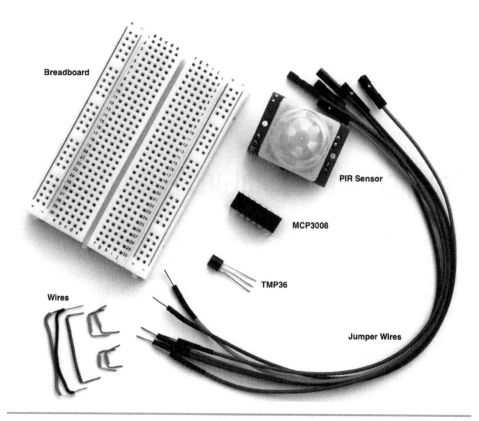

Figure 51—The parts you need

sensors and the MCP3008 chip. For example, Adafruit sells a PIR sensor (product ID 189), the TMP36 (product ID 165), and the MCP3008 (product ID 856). If you prefer the Parallax PIR sensor, make sure you're using Rev A.[1] The new version (Rev B) is a bit better, but its output voltage might be too high for the Pi. Also, Rev A costs less than five dollars at the moment and is sufficient for most purposes.

Make sure you buy the correct version of the MCP3008 chip, because they're available with different cases. You need the MCP3008-I/P (16 pins), because you can use it with a breadboard.

WARNING! Never attach a sensor that outputs more than 3.3V directly to the Pi. It will damage your Pi! Be very careful when buying new parts for the Pi.

---

1. Search for product number 910-28027 at http://www.parallax.com/

Detect Motion with the Pi

Chances are good that you benefit from motion detectors several times a week or even several times a day. They might turn on the lights automatically at dark, or perhaps they turn on the lights when you enter the restroom at work. In this section, you'll learn how these detectors work, and you'll learn how to turn the Pi into a motion detector.

Connect the PIR Sensor to the Pi

Many motion detectors use passive infrared (PIR) sensors.[2] A PIR sensor permanently measures infrared light and notices whenever something in the infrared spectrum changes. This is all you need to detect motion, because nearly every object emits infrared light. That's true for everything in front of your house: the ground, a bicycle, a garbage can, and so on. All of these things emit a fairly constant portion of infrared light, and it doesn't change rapidly. But if a human being or an animal approaches your front door, the sensor will notice a big variation and fire a signal.

The innards of PIR sensors are rather complex, but using them is easy. In the following figure, you can see the Parallax PIR sensor (Rev A) that we'll use in this section's examples. The sensor has a jumper you can use for changing its behavior. Make sure it's in position H; that is, the jumper covers the pin next to the H.[3]

Figure 52—Top and bottom of a passive infrared sensor

---

2. http://en.wikipedia.org/wiki/Passive_infrared_sensor
3. At http://www.ladyada.net/learn/sensors/pir.html, you'll find an excellent tutorial explaining all the sensor's details.

Also, the sensor has three pins that you need to connect to the Pi using female/male jumper wires. In the following figure, you can see how. Connect the Pi's 5V pin to the sensor's power pin and the Pi's ground pin to the sensor's ground pin. Finally, connect the sensor's signal pin to pin GPIO23 on the Pi. Usually, the pins on the sensor are labeled. When in doubt, look at the sensor's data sheet.

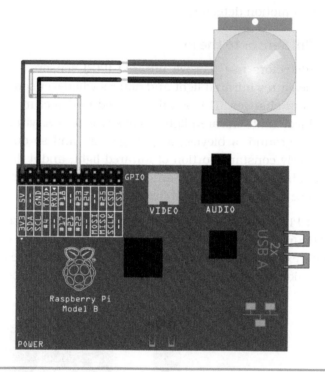

Figure 53—The PIR circuit

All digital PIR sensors work more or less the same way. As long as they don't detect motion, they don't output any current on their signal pin. When they detect motion, they output a high signal—that is, a certain current that you can usually look up in the sensor's data sheet.

WARNING AGAIN! Never attach a sensor that outputs more than 3.3V directly to the Pi. It will damage your Pi!

Control a PIR Sensor

Now that the wiring is finished, we have to control the sensor using some software. For many programming tasks on the Pi, the Python programming language[4] is a good choice. It's easy to learn, and the RPi library[5] has many convenient functions for controlling the Pi's GPIO pins. Raspbian already comes with Python, but you have to install RPi:

```
pi@raspberry:~$ sudo apt-get update
pi@raspberry:~$ sudo apt-get install python-dev python-rpi.gpio
```

That's all the preparation we need, and now we can define a new Python class for working with a PIR sensor:

```
Sensors/pir.py
Line 1  import RPi.GPIO as GPIO
     2  class PassiveInfraredSensor:
     3    def __init__(self, pin):
     4      self.pin = pin
     5      GPIO.setmode(GPIO.BCM)
     6      GPIO.setup(self.pin, GPIO.IN)
     7
     8    def motion_detected(self):
     9      return GPIO.input(self.pin)
```

Even if you've never worked with Python before, you should be able to understand most of the code. Before we dissect the code line by line, you should know that Python treats whitespace differently from most other programming languages. Instead of creating code blocks using curly braces ({ }) or keywords such as begin and end, Python uses indentation. It doesn't matter whether you use spaces or tabs to indent a block of code, but you have to be consistent. That is, if you've indented the first line of a block using four spaces, you have to indent the next line using four spaces, too.

In the first line we import RPi's GPIO functions, so we can use them in our own code. Then we define a new class named PassiveInfraredSensor. Whenever we create a new PassiveInfraredSensor object, Python will call the __init__() function. This function expects two arguments: the newly created object (self) and the number of the pin to which we've connected the sensor (pin). Python will initialize the first argument automatically.

In line 4, we store the pin number in the current object, and after that we set the numbering scheme for the pins using the GPIO.setmode() function. We pass it the value GPIO.BCM, so the RPi library interprets pin numbers using the Broadcom definition. (See the top and bottom rows in Figure 46, *The Pi's GPIO pins*, on page 95.) In our case, the pin number is 23 because we have connected the sensor's signal pin to pin GPIO23 on the Pi.

---

4. http://www.python.org/
5. http://code.google.com/p/raspberry-gpio-python/

Alternatively, we can set the mode to GPIO.BOARD. In this case, RPi interprets pin numbers as they are defined on the Raspberry Pi board, and we'd have to use 16 instead with our current setup. (See the two rows in Figure 46, *The Pi's GPIO pins*, on page 95, beginning with Pin.) Finally, we turn the pin to which the sensor is connected into an input pin by calling GPIO.setup() in line 6.

Then we define a method named motion_detected(). It calls GPIO.input(), passing it our signal pin number. Depending on the method call's result, it returns True if the sensor has detected a motion and False otherwise. Again, Python sets the self argument automatically for us.

Our PassiveInfraredSensor class is complete now, so let's use it to build a motion detector. The following program periodically checks whether the PIR sensor has detected motion. It prints a message if someone moves, and it also prints a message if nobody has moved for more than two seconds.

Sensors/pir_demo.py

```
Line 1  from pir import *
   -    import time
   -
   -    PIR_PIN = 23
   5    pir = PassiveInfraredSensor(PIR_PIN)
   -
   -    last_state = False
   -    while True:
   -        if (pir.motion_detected() == True):
   10           if (last_state == False):
   -                print "Movement detected"
   -                last_state = True
   -        else:
   -            if (last_state == True):
   15               print "No movement detected"
   -                time.sleep(2)
   -                last_state = False;
```

In the first two lines, we import the PassiveInfraredSensor class and Python's functions for manipulating dates and times. Then we define a constant named PIR_PIN and set it to the number of our signal pin. We use the constant in the following line when we create a new PassiveInfraredSensor object for the first time.

The detection algorithm starts in line 7. We store the last state of the PIR sensor in a variable named last_state. Then we start an endless loop and check to see whether the PIR sensor has currently detected a motion. If yes, we check whether this is a new motion or whether we have detected it before. If it is new, we print the message "Movement detected."

If the PIR sensor hasn't detected a motion, we check whether it has previously detected a motion. If it has, we print the message "No movement detected" and wait for two seconds until we start again. Overall, we make sure that we print a message only if the state has actually changed. This prevents our motion detector from looking a bit nervous.

Now run the program, move a little in front of the PIR sensor, and stand still from time to time.

```
pi@raspberry:~$ sudo python pir_demo.py
Movement detected
No movement detected
```

That's all you need to turn the Pi into a motion detector. Printing a message isn't very spectacular, but you can easily improve the program so that it sends an email or switches on a light. That way, you could turn your Pi into a burglar alarm or make it the basis of a home-automation system.

Attaching most digital sensors to the Pi is easy as long as their output voltage matches the Pi's specifications and as long as they don't depend on an accurate timing. Working with analog sensors can be more complicated, but in the next section you'll see that it isn't rocket science, either.

Measure Temperature with the Pi

Digital sensors have many applications and are easy to use, but in many cases analog sensors have some advantages. For example, most processes in nature are analog, so analog sensors are a better fit for measuring phenomena such as temperature or acceleration.

Analog sensors usually measure a certain parameter and output a voltage that corresponds to the size of their current input signal. For example, a temperature sensor such as the TMP36 outputs a higher voltage for higher temperatures and a lower voltage for lower temperatures.

Although this sounds reasonable and easy, we still have a problem: digital computers like the Raspberry Pi don't understand analog voltage signals. They can only interpret digital signals—that is, HIGH or LOW current. Microcontroller boards such as the Arduino have native support for analog signals because they have an analog-to-digital converter (A/D) that takes a voltage signal and turns it into a binary number. To achieve the same with the Raspberry Pi, we need to attach an A/D to the Pi.

Meet the MCP3008

The MCP3008[6] is an A/D that works great with the Pi. It's cheap, it's easy to use, and it can read up to eight analog signals at the same time. Its output resolution is 10 bits; that is, it returns numbers in the range of 0 to 1023 corresponding to the voltage signal emitted by an analog sensor. You can see the MCP3008's pins in the following figure.

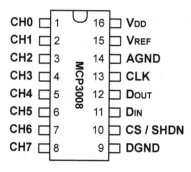

Figure 54—The pin layout of an MCP3008 A/D

You can use pins 1 to 8 on the left side to connect up to eight analog sensors. Half the pins on the right side are needed for the power supply and ground (VDD, VREF, AGND, and DGND). With the remaining four pins (CLK, DOUT, DIN, and CS), you can read the current voltage signal as a digital number.

The MCP3008 has a resolution of 10 bits, so you might be wondering how it's possible to transfer 10 bits using only four digital pins. You might expect the chip to have ten pins for emitting the value of the current analog signal. In theory that's a good idea, but adding ten pins would be wasteful. Not only would the MCP3008 need more pins, but the Pi would need more pins, too.

That's why the MCP3008 does something more sophisticated to output its readings. It implements the Serial Peripheral Interface (SPI).[7] SPI allows you to create a synchronous serial link between a master and several slaves. The master and slaves communicate via a serial bus; in our case, the Pi is the master and the MCP3008 is the slave. Whenever the Pi wants to read an analog signal, it sends a message to the MCP3008 and gets back a response. To establish an SPI bus between two devices, you need four wires.

6.   http://www.microchip.com/wwwproducts/Devices.aspx?dDocName=en010530
7.   http://en.wikipedia.org/wiki/Serial_Peripheral_Interface_Bus

In the following figure, you can see how to connect the Pi to the MCP3008 so they can communicate using SPI. (Don't worry! You'll see the rest of the wiring next.)

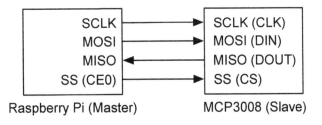

Raspberry Pi (Master)   MCP3008 (Slave)

Figure 55—This is how you connect two SPI devices.

Note that SPI isn't a very strict specification, so different vendors use different labels for their pins. With the SCLK line, the master and the slave synchronize their work using a common clock signal. The MOSI (Master Out, Slave In) line is for sending data from the master to the slave, while MISO (Master In, Slave Out) is for transferring data back from the slave to the master. Using the SS line (Slave Select), the master selects the slave it wants to do some work.

Implementing SPI communication in software isn't difficult, but the Pi's hardware supports it out of the box. The same is true for Raspbian. In the next section, you'll learn how to enable it.

Enable SPI on the Pi

By default, Raspbian doesn't enable SPI, so you need to either enable it using raspi-config (see *Enable the SPI Kernel Module*, on page 30) or adjust a few configuration files. If you're working with a recent version of Raspbian, you'll find an option named SPI in raspi-config's Advanced Options menu. Choose this option, enable SPI, and you're finished.

If you're working with an older release or prefer to enable SPI manually, you'll need to remove SPI from the module blacklist by editing /etc/modprobe.d/raspi-blacklist.conf:

```
pi@raspberry:~$ sudo nano /etc/modprobe.d/raspi-blacklist.conf
```

As of this writing, this file contains only two lines for disabling SPI and I^2C. It probably looks like this:

```
blacklist spi-bcm2708
blacklist i2c-bcm2708
```

To remove SPI support from the blacklist, you need to comment out the corresponding line so the file looks like this:

```
#blacklist spi-bcm2708
blacklist i2c-bcm2708
```

Alternatively, you can delete the line. Save the file and then add the SPI module to the list of modules the Pi loads automatically when it starts:

pi@raspberry:~$ **sudo nano /etc/modules**

Add a new line containing only the word spidev and save the file. Then reboot the Pi:

pi@raspberry:~$ **sudo reboot**

Now your Pi should support two SPI devices. You can look them up using the following command:

pi@raspberry:~$ **ls /dev/spidev***
```
/dev/spidev0.0  /dev/spidev0.1
```

In the next section, we'll bring one of these devices to life by connecting an MCP3008 and a temperature sensor to the Pi.

Wire It All Up

Now that we know how SPI works in principle, we need to connect the Pi to the MCP3008, and the MCP3008 to the TMP36 temperature sensor. In Figure 56, *The TMP36 circuit*, on page 117, you can see how to do this.

We need to connect the Pi's power and ground pins to a couple of places on the breadboard. So, we connect them to the two rows at the left of the breadboard. From there, we can easily distribute power and ground to other places using short wires.

Next we plug in the MCP3008 chip; we have to make sure it has the right orientation. Chips have a U notch at the top, and the MCP3008 is no exception. Pin 1 is to the left of the U notch. Gently plug it into the breadboard. You'll have to press firmly after you get them all lined up, but first double-check to ensure that all pins fit into their holes. Use a small screwdriver as a lever if you need to remove the chip.

Also, be very careful when wiring the MCP3008 to the Pi. Table 1, *Pin mapping for connecting the Pi to the MCP3008*, on page 117 explains in detail how to connect the Pi's GPIO pins to the MCP3008.

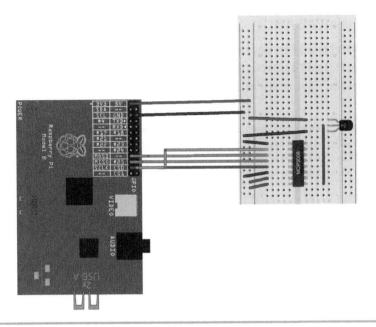

Figure 56—The TMP36 circuit

Raspberry Pi Pin	MCP3008 Pin
1 (3.3V)	16 (VDD)
1 (3.3V)	15 (VREF)
6 (GND)	14 (AGND)
6 (GND)	9 (DGND)
23 (SCLK)	13 (CLK)
21 (MISO)	12 (DOUT)
19 (MOSI)	11 (DIN)
24 (CE0)	10 (CS)

Table 1—Pin mapping for connecting the Pi to the MCP3008

Connecting the TMP36 sensor is easy because it has only three pins. Plug the sensor into the breadboard and make sure it has the correct orientation. Connect the sensor's power pin to the Pi's 3.3V pin and its ground pin to the Pi's ground. Then connect the TMP36's signal pin to pin 1 (CH0) of the MCP3008.

So, the wiring is finished. Now we need to write some software so that we can finally find out what the temperature is.

Control the MCP3008

The MCP3008 is an SPI device, so we need to find a way to communicate with it using the Pi's SPI hardware. Fortunately, several people have already done this. py-spidev[8] is a small library that provides everything we need. Install it as follows:

```
pi@raspberry:~$ sudo apt-get install python-dev python-rpi.gpio
pi@raspberry:~$ git clone git://github.com/doceme/py-spidev
pi@raspberry:~$ cd py-spidev
pi@raspberry:~$ sudo python setup.py install
```

The following is all we need to implement an MCP3008 class using Python:

Sensors/mcp3008.py

```
Line 1  import spidev
     -
     -  class MCP3008:
     -    def __init__(self, bus = 0, client = 0):
     5      self.spi = spidev.SpiDev()
     -      self.spi.open(bus, client)
     -
     -    def analog_read(self, channel):
     -      if (channel < 0 or channel > 7):
    10        return -1
     -      result = self.spi.xfer2([1, (8 + channel) << 4, 0])
     -      return ((result[1] & 3) << 8) + result[2]
```

It's just a short class, but it needs some explanation. In the first line we import the spidev library we installed before. Then we define a class named MCP3008. As before, in the PassiveInfrared class, we define a method named __init__() that will be called whenever we create a new MCP3008 object. __init__() expects three parameters: the newly created instance (self), the number of the SPI bus to be used (bus), and the number of the client (slave) we'd like to talk to (client). In line 5, we create a new SpiDev object, and we open a connection to the device in the following line.

So far we've only established a communication channel to an SPI device; that is, what we do in the __init__() method isn't specific to the MCP3008. It would be the same for every other SPI device. The specific parts happen in analog_read(). This method takes a port number and returns the current reading of the analog sensor that has been connected to the port. We check whether the port number is between 0 and 7, and if it's not we return −1.

---

8. https://github.com/doceme/py-spidev

In line 11, we send a message to the MCP3008 using the xfer2() method of our SpiDev object. xfer2() expects an array of bytes and sends it using the SPI protocol. In our case we need to send 3 bytes, and you might be wondering what their meaning is. You can find the answer in Chapters 5 and 6 of the MCP3008's data sheet.[9] The data sheet explains in detail what data the MCP3008 expects and what data it sends back. The structure of the input message looks like this:

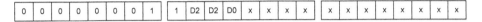

| 0 | 0 | 0 | 0 | 0 | 0 | 0 | 1 | | 1 | D2 | D2 | D0 | x | x | x | x | | x | x | x | x | x | x | x | x |

Most of the bits in these 3 bytes have a constant value. Only the 3 bits named D0, D1, and D2 may vary, and they contain the number of the channel you'd like to read. So the first byte is always 1, the last byte is always 0, and the second byte contains a slightly shifted version of the channel number. We set all bits marked with an x to 0.

The MCP3008's response message consists of 3 bytes, too. Their meaning is:

| ? | ? | ? | ? | ? | ? | ? | ? | | ? | ? | ? | ? | ? | 0 | B9 | B8 | | B7 | B6 | B5 | B4 | B3 | B2 | B1 | B0 |

Only the lower 10 bits are interesting; ignore the rest. Line 12 extracts the interesting bits and returns them as a single number.

With the MCP3008 class, it's easy to read the current temperature:

Sensors/tmp36_demo.py
```
Line 1  from mcp3008 import *
    -   import time
    -
    -   mcp = MCP3008()
    5   TMP36_CHANNEL = 0
    -
    -   while True:
    -       analog_value = mcp.analog_read(TMP36_CHANNEL)
    -       voltage = 3.3 * analog_value / 1024
   10       temperature_c = (voltage * 1000 - 500) / 10
    -       temperature_f = 9.0 / 5.0 * temperature_c + 32.0
    -       print "Temperature: %.1fC (%.1fF)" % (temperature_c, temperature_f)
    -       time.sleep(1)
```

After importing the MCP3008 class and Python's time functions, we create a new MCP3008 object in line 4. We also define a constant for the channel to which we connected the TMP36 sensor.

---

9. http://ww1.microchip.com/downloads/en/DeviceDoc/21295d.pdf

We start an endless loop and read the TMP36's current value by calling analog_read(). In line 9, we turn this value into the actual voltage emitted by the sensor. The following line calculates the actual temperature in degrees Celsius using a formula you can find by studying the sensor's data sheet.[10] We convert this value into degrees Fahrenheit, too, and print them both. Then we wait for a second and measure the current temperature again.

Run the program, and its output should look like this:

```
pi@raspberry:~$ sudo python tmp36_demo.py
Temperature: 20.9C (69.6F)
Temperature: 20.9C (69.6F)
```

And we're finished! We can measure the current temperature with the Pi. You've not only learned how to attach an analog sensor to the Pi, you've also learned how to work with SPI devices—which is great, because they're very popular.

What If It Doesn't Work?

All the advice from *What If It Doesn't Work?*, on page 105, also applies to the projects in this chapter. In addition, you have to be very careful when plugging the MCP3008 into the breadboard. Make sure you don't bend any of its pins accidentally. You also need to double-check every single connection from the MCP3008 to the Pi.

Take a close look at the pins of the PIR sensor and the TMP36, too. Not all PIR sensors have the same order of pins, and you can easily mix up the pins of the TMP36.

Next Steps

You've learned how to work with digital and analog sensors, and you've learned how to control SPI devices. The Pi also supports I^2C,[11] which is another popular standard for connecting devices. It's certainly a good idea to look at it.

If you'd like to build more ambitious projects, you should consider buying an extension board for the Pi. For example, the Adafruit Prototyping Pi Plate[12] makes prototyping much easier. The Gertboard[13] makes prototyping even safer, and it comes with a lot of nice features, too.

---

10. http://www.analog.com/static/imported-files/data_sheets/TMP35_36_37.pdf
11. http://en.wikipedia.org/wiki/I%C2%B2C
12. http://adafruit.com/products/801
13. http://www.raspberrypi.org/archives/411

CHAPTER 11

Control the Pi Camera

One of the greatest advantages of the Pi's homogeneous hardware is that it's easy to build new accessories for it. The Raspberry Pi team has had a CSI (Camera Serial Interface) slot on the board from the beginning, and they recently released a camera module.

The camera is tiny but powerful. You can use it to take high-definition photos and record videos. Its small size, low weight, and modest power consumption make it an ideal candidate for many interesting projects. For example, you can attach it to a remote-controlled quadcopter to record some videos of your latest maneuvers.

In this chapter, you'll learn how to connect the camera to the Pi and how to get it up and running. You'll use simple command-line tools to take photos and record videos. Also, you'll build an automatic burglar alarm using the camera and a PIR sensor.

Meet the Camera's Hardware

The Pi camera module is very small: 24mm x 25mm. Its height is 9mm, and it weighs only about 3 grams. Like the Pi, it doesn't look very pretty (see Figure 57, *The camera's design is similar to the Pi's*, on page 122), but like the Pi it's surprisingly powerful and versatile.

In most regards, the camera is similar to the cameras you can find in modern smartphones. It has a fixed-focus lens that captures photos at a resolution of 2592 x 1944 pixels. It supports three video modes with different resolutions and frame rates: 1080p at 30 FPS, 720p at 60 FPS, and 640 x 480 at 60 or 90 FPS.

Figure 57—The camera's design is similar to the Pi's.

Connect the Camera to the Pi

Connecting the camera module to the Pi isn't difficult, but working with the CSI port is a bit unusual compared to connecting USB devices, for example. Before you can plug in the camera, you have to open the CSI connector by pulling it up a little bit. Hold the Raspberry Pi board with one hand, grasp the connector between the thumb and forefinger of your other hand, and pull it up a few millimeters. Then insert the camera's cable carefully while the cable's contacts point to the HDMI connector. Finally, close the CSI connector by pressing it firmly from above. In Figure 58, *Connecting the camera is easy but a bit unusual*, on page 123, you can see how to connect the camera module correctly.

To make the camera work, you have to install some drivers; you'll learn how to do that in the next section.

Install the Camera Drivers

The latest version of Raspbian includes all the camera drivers. If you don't run the latest version, you'll have to update your software stack. Issue the following commands:

```
$ sudo apt-get update
$ sudo apt-get upgrade -y
$ sudo apt-get install git-core -y
$ sudo wget http://goo.gl/1BOfJ -O /usr/bin/rpi-update
$ sudo chmod +x /usr/bin/rpi-update
$ sudo rpi-update
```

Figure 58—Connecting the camera is easy but a bit unusual.

These commands install the latest firmware and camera drivers for your Pi. Also, you have to run raspi-config to enable the camera (see *Enable the Pi Camera*, on page 29) and set the GPU memory to 128MB (see *Adjust the Pi's Memory Layout*, on page 30).

In addition to the drivers, you get a few useful command-line tools for taking photos and videos. In the next sections, you'll learn how to use them.

Take Some Photos

After you've connected the camera and installed the drivers, it's easy to take some photos. The tool for the job is raspistill. When you call it without any arguments, it prints a long list of options.

```
$ raspistill
```

Before we play with the options, let's take an initial test photo. Run the following command and point the camera to something that looks interesting.

```
$ raspistill -o first.jpg
```

This command will take a photo and write it to a file named first.jpg. Before the camera actually captures the photo, it'll show a preview on the screen for five seconds. Note that you don't have to start a graphical desktop environment to work with the camera. It will work just fine using a plain text terminal.

If you'd like to take a photo immediately—that is, without a five-second delay— you have to run the following command:

```
$ raspistill -t 0 -o first.jpg
```

With the -t option, we can set the delay in milliseconds. When we set it to 0, raspistill doesn't show a preview window. If you'd like to have a delay but you want to disable the preview window, you have to set the -n option.

```
$ raspistill -t 2000 -n -o first.jpg
```

In this case, raspistill will wait for two seconds before taking a photo, but it won't show the preview window. We can adjust the preview window's size in a couple of ways. We can make it occupy the entire screen, and we can set it to an arbitrary size.

You might've noticed that the photos you've taken so far have been flipped horizontally. Using -hf, we can change this behavior:

```
$ raspistill -hf -o first.jpg
```

Setting the -vf option flips the photo vertically. Note that raspistill doesn't show a preview when we're using the flipping options. It only shows the final result before writing it to a file.

Usually the JPEG format is a good choice for storing photos, but sometimes you might need a different format. Using the -e option, we can set the output file encoding to JPG, PNG, BMP, or GIF. For example, the following command stores a photo in PNG format:

```
$ raspistill -e PNG -o first.png
```

In addition, you can choose from various effects that you're probably used to from your regular camera. Using the options -ex, -ifx, and -awd, you can adjust the camera to different lightings and generate popular effects.

Create Time-Lapse Videos

One of the greatest advantages of the Pi camera module over most regular cameras is that you can automate it. For example, it's very easy to use it to create time-lapse videos. Although you could write a program that automatically calls raspistill every few seconds, raspistill supports time-lapsing right out of the box.

```
$ mkdir photos
$ raspistill -n -tl 3000 -t 600000 -o photos/photo%04d.jpg
```

The preceding command takes a photo every three seconds (3,000 milliseconds) for ten minutes (600,000 milliseconds). It stores all photos in a folder named photos, and all filenames start with the prefix "photo" followed by a four-digit number. raspistill does the numbering automatically, so in the photos folder, you'll find files named photo0001.jpg, photo0002.jpg, and so on.

Now we have to combine the photo files into a single video file. Several free tools are available for this job. FFmpeg[1] and avconv[2] are very popular because they're extremely powerful.

In theory, you can install and run both tools on the Pi, but it's usually best to install just avconv, for a couple of reasons. To install FFmpeg, you have to compile it yourself, which is a bit inconvenient. Also FFmpeg and avconv are very similar because avconv is a fork of the FFmpeg project.

```
$ sudo apt-get install libav-tools
```

Then we can create a time-lapse video using the following command:

```
$ cd photos
$ avconv -r 4 -i photo%04d.jpg -r 4 -vcodec libx264 -crf 20 -g 15 video.mp4
```

avconv has a huge number of command-line options, and we can control every single aspect of the generated video file. Run man avconv to read the program's manual.

Generating videos consumes a lot of resources, and it literally takes hours to generate a video on the Pi itself. The best solution is to copy the photo files to a more powerful computer. Then you can use ffmpeg to generate the video:

```
$ cd photos
$ ffmpeg -qscale 5 -r 4 -b 9600 -i photo%04d.jpg video.mp4
```

After running this command, you'll find a video file named video.mp4 in the photos folder. Like avconv, ffmpeg supports a vast number of options, and you can look them up by running man ffmpeg.

raspistill is an amazingly versatile tool, and even though you've learned about many of its options, there are still more to explore. Don't be shy—go ahead and play around with them.

Record High-Definition Videos

raspistill is probably all you'll ever need to take photos with the Pi camera module, but you can't use it to record videos. That's what raspivid is for, and it supports nearly the same set of options as raspistill.

To record one minute (60,000 milliseconds) of high-definition video using 25 frames per second, run the following command:

```
$ raspivid -t 60000 -fps 25 -o video.h264
```

---

1.   http://www.ffmpeg.org/

2.   http://libav.org/avconv.html

This results in a file named video.h264 that contains the video data encoded using the H.264 codec. This codec is popular, but to make it work with most video players we have to put it into a suitable container, like MP4:

```
$ avconv -r 25 -i video.h264 -vcodec copy video.mp4
```

Now video.mp4 contains an MP4 version of our video that we can play using nearly any video player in the world.

All in all, the Pi camera produces good videos. The only thing that's missing is a microphone. Still, you can create many useful and fun projects with it. In the next section, you'll learn how to build a burglar alarm using the camera and a motion detector.

Build a Burglar Alarm

In *Detect Motion with the Pi*, on page 109, you learned how to control a motion sensor with the Pi. The controlling software only printed messages to the console—which is fine for demonstration purposes, but in real life it's not very useful. In this section, you'll learn how to build an actual burglar alarm that takes photos automatically as soon as someone moves, and then sends an email with the latest photo attached.

Disable the Camera's LED

A burglar alarm should work as unobtrusively as possible, and one feature of the Pi camera contradicts this principle. Whenever the camera takes a photo or records a video, it turns on a bright-red LED. Usually this is good because it shows that the camera is working and it prevents you from taking pictures of people secretly. However, for a burglar alarm we should disable the LED.

We could simply hide it under some duct tape, but that wouldn't be very elegant. The Raspbian team provided an option to disable the camera LED completely. Open the file /boot/config.txt using the nano text editor, for example:

```
$ sudo nano /boot/config.txt
```

Add the following line at the end of the file:

```
disable_camera_led=1
```

Finally, reboot the Pi:

```
$ sudo reboot
```

Now the Pi camera won't turn on the LED when it takes pictures or records videos. We can still control the LED via our own software, as you'll learn in the next paragraphs.

Control the Camera Using Python

For the burglar alarm, we need to find a way to take photos programmatically. That is, we need to write some software to control the camera.

In *Detect Motion with the Pi*, on page 109, we wrote the code for controlling the PIR sensor in Python, so it's advantageous to write the code for controlling the camera in Python, too. It would also be great if we could reuse the raspistill code so we don't have to reinvent the wheel.[3]

The easiest way to integrate raspistill with Python is to execute the command-line utility using Python's subprocess module. in most cases, invoking command-line tools from programming languages isn't an ideal solution because of poor performance. In this case it's OK, because taking pictures takes some time, so the overhead of creating a subshell is negligible. All we need is the following Camera class:

camera/camera.py

```
Line 1   import RPi.GPIO as GPIO
    -    from subprocess import call
    -
    -    CameraLedPin = 5
    5
    -    class Camera:
    -      def __init__(self):
    -        GPIO.setmode(GPIO.BCM)
    -        GPIO.setwarnings(False)
   10        GPIO.setup(CameraLedPin, GPIO.OUT, initial = False)
    -
    -      def led_on(self):
    -        GPIO.output(CameraLedPin, True)
    -
   15      def led_off(self):
    -        GPIO.output(CameraLedPin, False)
    -
    -      def take_photo(self, filename):
    -        call(['raspistill -n -t 0 -hf -o {0}'.format(filename)], shell = True)
```

It's not a lot of code, and its most complicated parts don't deal with taking pictures, but instead with controlling the camera's LED. The __init__() method prepares the LED's control pin in lines 7 to 10. The LED is hardwired to GPIO

---

3. You can find a Python library for the Pi camera at https://github.com/waveform80/picamera/.

pin number 5, so we can easily turn it on and off using led_on() and led_off(), respectively.

Using the take_photo() method, we can take a new photo, and the method will delegate its work to raspistill. It sets a few reasonable defaults that we can change easily. The following program shows how to use the Camera class:

camera/camera_demo.py
```
from camera import *
camera = Camera()
camera.led_off()
camera.take_photo('photo.jpg')
```

This small demo program includes the Camera class and creates a new instance named camera. Then it turns off the camera's LED and takes a new photo. It stores the photo in a file named photo.jpg.

Now that we can control the camera from a Python program, we need a way to send an email with a photo attachment. You'll learn how to do that in the next section.

Send an Email

Sending emails programmatically is no big deal using modern programming languages, and Python is no exception. It has great support for SMTP,[4] and it supports email attachments in various forms. The following EmailNotification class provides all the functionality for sending emails with photo attachments:

camera/email_notification.py
```
import smtplib
from email.mime.image import MIMEImage
from email.mime.multipart import MIMEMultipart

class EmailNotification:
  def __init__(self, server, user, pwd):
    self.server = server
    self.user = user
    self.pwd = pwd
    self.subject = 'INTRUDER ALERT!'
    self.from_addr = 'me@example.com'
    self.to_addr = 'alert@example.com'

  def send(self, image_file):
    msg = MIMEMultipart()
    msg['Subject'] = self.subject
    msg['From'] = self.from_addr
    msg['To'] = self.to_addr
```

---

4. http://en.wikipedia.org/wiki/Simple_Mail_Transfer_Protocol

```
    msg.preamble = self.subject
    msg.attach(self.__read_image(image_file))
    self.__send_email(msg)

  def __read_image(self, image_file):
    attachment = open(image_file, 'rb')
    image_data = MIMEImage(attachment.read())
    attachment.close()
    return image_data

  def __send_email(self, msg):
    server = smtplib.SMTP(self.server)
    server.ehlo()
    server.starttls()
    server.login(self.user, self.pwd)
    server.sendmail(self.from_addr, self.to_addr, msg.as_string())
    server.quit()
```

The __init__() method initializes the name of your SMTP server, its username, and its password. Also, it defines the default subject of your email, its origin address, and its recipient. You're free to change all of them.

Using the send() method, we can send an image file via email. The method creates a new MIMEMultipart object containing all of the email's properties, including an image file that has been created using the Pi camera.

Finally, __send_email() sends an email using Python's smptlib. Depending on your current email provider, you might have to adjust this method. For example, some providers insist on the call to ehlo() and others don't.

Build the Final Product

We now have software to control the PIR sensor and the Pi camera, and we're able to send emails. The only thing left to do is to combine all the single parts into a complete burglar alarm.

Using the PassiveInfraredSensor, Camera, and EmailNotification classes, it's easy to build a burglar alarm:

camera/burglar_alarm.py
```
Line 1  from pir import *
     -  from camera import *
     -  from email_notification import *
     -  import time
     5
     -  PIR_PIN = 23
     -  PREFIX = 'photos/alert'
     -  EMAIL_SERVER = 'smtp.gmail.com:587'
     -  EMAIL_USER = 'me@example.com'
```

```
10  EMAIL_PWD = 't0p$ecret'

 -  pir = PassiveInfraredSensor(PIR_PIN)
 -  camera = Camera()
 -  notifier = EmailNotification(EMAIL_SERVER, EMAIL_USER, EMAIL_PWD)
15  i = 0
 -  last_state = False
 -  while True:
 -      if (pir.motion_detected() == True):
 -          if (last_state == False):
20              print 'INTRUDER ALERT!'
 -              image_file = PREFIX + '{0}.jpg'.format(i)
 -              camera.take_photo(image_file)
 -              notifier.send(image_file)
 -              i = i + 1
25              last_state = True
 -      else:
 -          if (last_state == True):
 -              time.sleep(1)
 -              last_state = False;
```

In lines 7 to 10, we define the most important attributes of the burglar alarm. Simply insert your email provider's SMTP server, your username, and your password.

The rest of the program works exactly like the motion detector in *Detect Motion with the Pi*, on page 109. Instead of simply printing a message to the console, it takes a photo and sends it via email in lines 21 to 23.

What If It Doesn't Work?

If you have any problems with the PIR sensor, take a look at *What If It Doesn't Work?*, on page 120. Attaching the camera is unusual but not a big deal. Still, if it isn't working, check to be sure you've plugged in the cable correctly.

The Pi camera is a great tool and toy for many purposes. Its main advantage is that you can easily control it programmatically. It's a perfect tool for creating time-lapse videos of your latest birthday party or for turning it into a dashboard camera in your car. It also can be the basis for a burglar alarm, but it works best in well-lighted environments.

Where to Go from Here

At this point you have learned what a versatile tool the Raspberry Pi is. You've learned how to install various operating systems and how to use the Pi as a day-to-day computer. In addition, you turned the Pi into a web server, and then you turned it into a multimedia center. On top of that, you've used it as a basis for electronics projects and attached digital and analog sensors.

The Pi is a much more open platform than most regular PCs. For example, you can easily create your own hardware extensions using the Pi's GPIO parts. Along with its friendly and active community, the Pi will be one of the most popular, useful, and fun gadgets in the years ahead. People publish useful projects every day, and there's no reason why you shouldn't create something special with the Pi, too.

A Linux Primer

The most popular operating system for the Pi is Linux, especially the Debian Linux distribution (Raspbian). If you've worked exclusively with operating systems such as Windows or Mac OS X until now, Linux might produce a little culture shock for you, mainly because on Linux systems the graphical user interface (GUI) is optional. That means you can run a Linux system without using a mouse and without double-clicking colorful icons.

Still, you need a way to interact with the system, and on Linux you have to use a shell for this purpose. A *shell* is a program that awaits your commands via a keyboard and passes them to the operating system (Linux). After Linux has run the command, the shell passes the results back to you.

The shell itself runs in a terminal that goes back to the very beginnings of computing. In these times, you had to connect to the "real" computers using a more or less dumb terminal that basically forwarded your inputs and displayed the computer's outputs. Today you no longer have to use explicit terminal devices, but the metaphor still lives on, and Linux depends on it.

So, whenever you log into a Linux computer, it usually starts a shell in a terminal session. In the shell, you can invoke commands that actually run on the Linux computer.

Nowadays, Linux comes with graphical desktop systems that are very similar to Windows and Mac OS X. Still, these desktop systems ship with a terminal emulator you can use to invoke commands directly. The LXDE desktop, for example, comes with a desktop emulator named LXTerminal. You can find a shortcut on the LXDE desktop, so double-click it, and the Pi will start a new terminal session.

A First Encounter

After you've logged into the Pi or after you've started a new terminal from the desktop, you'll see the following prompt awaiting your commands:

```
pi@raspberrypi ~ $
```

It doesn't look like much, but it already gives you a lot of information. For example, the first part (pi@raspberrypi) tells you that the host name of your computer is raspberrypi. It also tells you that your username is pi. This is an important piece of information, because Linux is a multiuser operating system. This means that multiple people can work on the same computer simultaneously (over a network, for example). Also, you can switch to another user account whenever you need to, so it's good to know who you are at the moment.

The next part of the prompt contains the file system path you're currently in. Here it consists only of the tilde character (~), which is an abbreviation for the user's home directory. Every Linux user has a home directory for storing personal data and configuration files. It's similar to the My Documents folder on Windows or the Documents folder on Mac OS X. The dollar sign at the end marks the end of the prompt.

To see the content of the current directory, type *ls* and press the Enter key to run the ls command.

```
pi@raspberrypi ~ $ ls
Desktop  python_games
```

The current directory contains two items named Desktop and python_games. From only their names, you cannot tell whether they are regular files or directories. Fortunately, you can control the behavior of most Linux commands using command options. Usually, these options consist of only a single letter preceded by a dash. The ls command supports many options, and when you pass it the -l (short for "long") option, it displays more information about the files in the current directory.

```
pi@raspberrypi ~ $ ls -l
total 8
drwxr-xr-x 2 pi pi 4096 Jul 15 19:36 Desktop
drwxr-xr-x 2 pi pi 4096 Jul 15 19:36 python_games
```

At first it looks a bit scary, but it's really easy to understand. For every item in the directory, ls displays the information shown in the following figure.

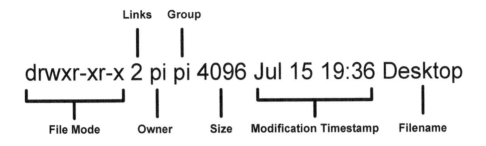

Figure 59—The different components of ls output

The file mode contains the file type and its permissions. If the first character is a dash, the file is a regular file. If it contains a *d*, it is a directory. So, both Desktop and python_games are directories.

The following nine characters encode the file permissions of three groups of people: the owner, the group, and others. The first three characters are rwx, and they mean that the owner of the file is allowed to read (r), write (w), and execute (x) it. In case of a directory, execute means to enter the directory.

Every file on a Linux system belongs to a user and to a group. Groups help to build teams who work together on the same resources. So, for every file, Linux stores permissions for the group, too. In the current case, they are r-x, which means that group members can read and execute the file but aren't allowed to change it.

Finally, Linux stores permissions for other users who are not a file's owner and who don't belong to the file's group. Again, r-x means that other users might read and execute the file but aren't allowed to change it.

The next information ls outputs is the number of links to a file. For your first tour through Linux, you can safely ignore it.

Then you can find the name of the file's owner and its group. In this case, both are pi; that is, on the current Linux system, there's both a user named pi and a group named pi.

Next you can find the file size. On Linux, directories are files too, and they simply contain the names of the files stored in the directory. By default, Linux allocates some space for this list of files up front, and in case of Debian on the Raspberry Pi, it's 4,096 bytes.

To the right of the file size, you can see the date the file was modified for the last time. And, finally, ls outputs the file's name.

Navigate Through the File System

The pwd (print working directory) command outputs the directory you're currently in.

```
pi@raspberrypi ~ $ pwd
/home/pi
```

As you can see, your home directory (~) expands to the absolute path /home/pi. Linux distinguishes between absolute and relative paths. Absolute paths always begin with a forward slash (/) and reference the same file no matter where you are in the file system. Relative paths, on the contrary, are relative to your current position in the file system. The following example will clarify the difference between absolute and relative paths.

As you saw in the preceding section, the pi user's home directory contains two directories named Desktop and python_games.

```
pi@raspberrypi ~ $ ls
Desktop    python_games
```

Using the cd (change directory) command, you can change the current directory to another one.

```
pi@raspberrypi ~ $ cd Desktop/
pi@raspberrypi ~/Desktop $
```

Now your current working directory has changed. You can see that your prompt has changed, and you can also check it using the pwd command.

```
pi@raspberrypi ~/Desktop $ pwd
/home/pi/Desktop
```

To go back to the pi user's home directory, you have a couple of options. First, you can invoke cd with the absolute path to the home directory.

```
pi@raspberrypi ~/Desktop $ cd /home/pi
pi@raspberrypi ~ $
```

Alternatively, you can use a relative path like this:

```
pi@raspberrypi ~/Desktop $ cd ..
pi@raspberrypi ~ $ pwd
/home/pi
```

The abbreviation .. stands for the parent directory of the current directory. In the previous command, your current working directory is /home/pi/Desktop. When you run cd .., you change the working directory to the parent directory of Desktop, which is /home/pi.

You can move to your user's home directory from any location in the file system by running cd with no arguments:

```
pi@raspberrypi ~/Desktop $ cd
pi@raspberrypi ~ $ pwd
/home/pi
```

This command is really useful, so it's worth remembering.

Edit Text Files

Many Linux tools depend on configuration files. Most of these files are regular text files, and you have to edit them from time to time. On Linux, you'll find many powerful text editors for the terminal. If you're used to graphical text editors, most Linux text editors look a bit awkward at first. One of the easiest and most intuitive editors is nano. It permanently displays shortcuts to its most important commands so you don't have to remember them. The following command starts nano and creates an empty text file named hello.txt:

```
pi@raspberrypi ~ $ nano hello.txt
```

In the following figure, you can see how nano looks in your terminal.

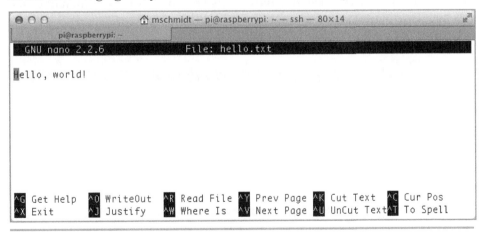

Figure 60—nano on the terminal

You can use most of the screen for editing the text, so type in a few words and move the cursor around using the cursor keys. At the bottom of the screen, you'll see the most important nano commands. To invoke them, you have to press the Ctrl key and the letter belonging to the command.

(The ^ character is an abbreviation for the Ctrl key.) For example, you can exit nano by pressing Ctrl+X.

When you do this, nano doesn't simply discard your changes and exit. It asks you whether you'd like to save your changes (see the following figure).

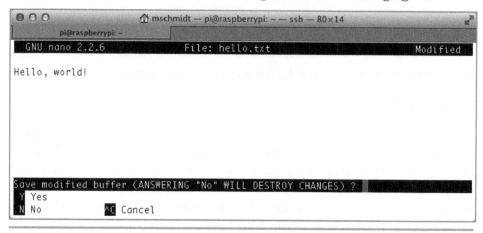

Figure 61—Saving a file with the nano text editor

Enter *y* if you'd like to save your changes and *n* otherwise. If you pressed *y*, you aren't finished yet, because nano asks you to confirm the filename (see the following figure).

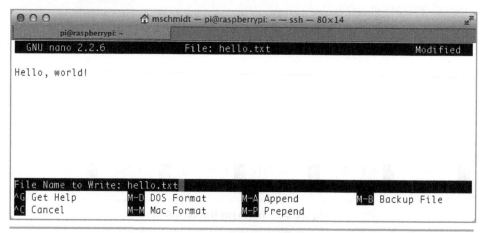

Figure 62—nano always asks you to confirm the filename.

Usually, you'll just press Enter to confirm the current filename, and nano will save the file. At the bottom of the screen, you can see some useful options allowing you to store the file in different formats, for example.

If you're going to work with Linux more often, you should get familiar with one of its text editors. For beginners, nano is an excellent choice, so play around with it for at least a few minutes.

Manage Users

Linux is a multiuser operating system—you can work with several different users on the same computer at the same time. In this book, you'll mainly use the user pi, because it comes with the Raspbian image automatically. This is convenient, but sometimes it's handy to create different users for different tasks. Also, pi is a very powerful user that has full administrative rights and can change nearly every aspect of the system. You don't want to grant all privileges to all users. It's always a good idea to work with only the administrative rights you need to get the job done. That way, you can't harm the system by accident.

Adding a new user to Linux is easy using the adduser command.

```
pi@raspberrypi ~ $ sudo adduser maik
❮ Adding user `maik' ...
  Adding new group `maik' (1002) ...
  Adding new user `maik' (1002) with group `maik' ...
  Creating home directory `/home/maik' ...ß
  Copying files from `/etc/skel' ...
  Enter new UNIX password:
  Retype new UNIX password:
  passwd: password updated successfully
  Changing the user information for maik
  Enter the new value, or press ENTER for the default
⇒   Full Name []: Maik Schmidt
❮   Room Number []:
    Work Phone []:
    Home Phone []:
    Other []:
⇒ Is the information correct? [Y/n] Y
```

You have to provide only a username (by convention it should contain only lowercase letters), a password, and a few optional attributes, such as your full name. After you've confirmed that all information is correct, Linux will create a new user with its own home directory. The next time you boot the Pi, you can use it to log into the system. If you're impatient, you can use the su (substitute user identity) command to switch to the new user.

```
pi@raspberrypi ~ $ su - maik
Password:
maik@raspberrypi ~ $ pwd
/home/maik
maik@raspberrypi ~ $ startx
```

su asks for the user's password, and if it's correct, it switches to the new user. The pwd command prints the current working directory; in this case, it's the home directory of the newly created user. If you start the LXDE desktop with the startx command, it greets you with the standard LXDE background image (see the following figure), because in contrast to the pi user, the new user starts with the desktop's defaults.

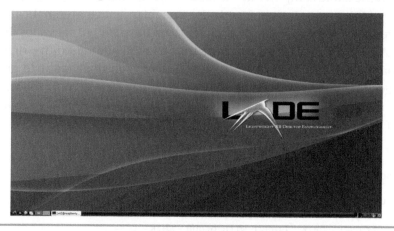

Figure 63—The default look of LXDE

When working with the pi user, you've often used sudo to run commands with administrative privileges. See what happens if you try to delete a file that you don't own using the rm (remove file) command.

```
maik@raspberrypi ~ $ sudo rm /boot/config.txt

We trust you have received the usual lecture from the local System
Administrator. It usually boils down to these three things:

    #1) Respect the privacy of others.
    #2) Think before you type.
    #3) With great power comes great responsibility.

[sudo] password for maik:
maik is not in the sudoers file.  This incident will be reported.
```

The command prints a warning and then asks for your password. Obviously, the new user isn't allowed to delete files in the /boot directory, so Linux refuses to invoke the rm command.

While it's a good default behavior to deny new users access to dangerous operations, sometimes users need more privileges. If you want to give your new users the same rights as the pi user, you have to add the user to the sudoers file. This file contains a list of all users who are allowed to run the sudo command, and it specifies which operations the users are allowed to perform. You can't edit the sudoers file directly; you have to use the visudo command, which invokes the text editor vi by default. If you want to edit the file using a different text editor, such as nano, you have to specify it on the command line. (Make sure you're using the pi user again.)

pi@raspberrypi ~ $ **sudo EDITOR=nano visudo**

This opens the /etc/sudoers file using the nano text editor. In the file, you'll find a section that looks like this:

```
# User privilege specification
root  ALL=(ALL) ALL
suse  ALL=(ALL) ALL
pi    ALL=(ALL) ALL
```

Add a new line that looks exactly like one of the previous three lines, but replace the username with the name of your new user. If you're using nano to edit the file, press Ctrl+X and confirm that you'd like to save the changes. Then confirm the filename, and you're finished—your new user now has the same rights as the original pi user.

If you no longer need a certain user, it's reasonable to delete it.

pi@raspberrypi ~ $ **sudo userdel maik**

The previous command will delete the user's account but not the user's files. The user can no longer log into the system, but all the files he or she has created in the home directory are still available. If you want to delete the files as well, run the following:

pi@raspberrypi ~ $ **sudo userdel -r maik**

If you ever need to change a user's attributes, such as his or her home directory, you can use the usermod command. You can use it to lock or unlock accounts, for example.

pi@raspberrypi ~ $ **sudo usermod -L maik**

This will lock the account of the user named maik. The user can no longer log into the system. To unlock the account, run the following command:

```
pi@raspberrypi ~ $ sudo usermod -U maik
```

You can read usermod's manual page (and the manual page of every other Linux command) using the man command.

```
pi@raspberrypi ~ $ man usermod
```

This displays the command's manual pages. You can stop the man command by pressing Q.

One important action is changing a user's password. For this, you can use the passwd command.

```
pi@raspberrypi ~ $ passwd maik
Changing password for maik.
Old Password:
New Password:
Retype New Password:
```

passwd asks for the current password and then for the new password. If everything is OK, it prints no message, and your user has a new password.

Manage Processes

Whenever you run a command or an application on a Linux system, the operating system's kernel spawns a new process. You can list your current processes using the ps command.

```
pi@raspberrypi ~ $ ps
  PID TTY          TIME CMD
 1880 pts/2    00:00:00 bash
 1892 pts/2    00:00:00 ps
```

At the moment, you own only two processes. The first has the process ID (PID) 1880, and it belongs to a command named bash. (The process IDs on your system will vary.) This is the process that belongs to the shell in which you're currently working. The process with the PID 1892 belongs to the ps command you've used to list your current processes. At the moment, you see the output of the ps command; process 1892 will be gone already. To see the effect, run ps again.

```
pi@raspberrypi ~ $ ps
  PID TTY          TIME CMD
 1880 pts/2    00:00:00 bash
 1894 pts/2    00:00:00 ps
```

As you can see, the shell still has the PID 1880, but your latest call to ps was handled by a new process with PID 1894.

You can get more information about your processes using the -f option.

```
pi@raspberrypi ~ $ ps -f
UID         PID  PPID  C STIME TTY          TIME CMD
pi         1880  1879  0 12:51 pts/2    00:00:00 -bash
pi         1895  1880  0 12:58 pts/2    00:00:00 ps -f
```

Now you can see the user ID (UID) of the user who has spawned a certain process. Not surprisingly, the UID is pi for all of your processes. In addition to the PID, you can see the parent process ID (PPID). This is the ID of the process that has created another process. For example, the ps -f command you've run before has the PPID 1880. This is the PID of the shell you're using. So, the shell is the parent of the process created by the ps -f command.

To see all information about all processes currently running on your Pi, run the following command:

```
pi@raspberrypi ~ $ ps -ef
```

This will output a fairly long list of processes that contains every single Linux service your Pi has started.

Getting a list of all active processes is useful, but most often you'll be looking for a certain process for a reason. Perhaps the process uses too many resources or takes too long, and you'd like to terminate it. But how can you terminate a process?

Terminating a long-running process is easy when you start it directly from the shell. To demonstrate, the following command searches for all text files on your SD card, so it will take a long time to finish:

```
pi@raspberrypi ~ $ find / -name '*.txt'
```

While the process is running, you can terminate it by pressing Ctrl+C on your keyboard. When you press Ctrl+C, the shell recognizes your keypress and sends a signal to the process that is currently running. Signals are small messages that all processes listen for in the background. Pressing Ctrl+C generates a signal named SIGINT that tells a process it got interrupted. When a process receives a SIGINT signal, it usually cleans up and terminates.

For processes that are still running in your terminal, pressing Ctrl+C is a good option, but what if you need to terminate a process that is running in the background? For example, most Linux services run in the background by default, and you don't start them yourself. In this case, you have to find out the PID of the process and pass it to the kill command.

```
pi@raspberrypi ~ $ kill 4711
```

The previous command sends the SIGTERM command to the process with the ID 4711. You can send other signals with the kill command, too. For example, the following command will terminate the process with the PID 4711 in any case:

```
pi@raspberrypi ~ $ kill -KILL 4711
```

Of course, you need to have the permission to terminate a process. Usually you are allowed to kill only your own processes.

Shut Down and Reboot the Pi

When you're finished with your work, don't simply switch off the Pi. It might result in the loss of data. Always shut it down using the following command:

```
pi@raspberrypi ~ $ sudo halt
```

If you need to reboot the Pi, use the following command:

```
pi@raspberrypi ~ $ sudo reboot
```

Get Help

Since their beginnings, the Unix/Linux operating systems came with a great manual system named *man pages*. Whenever you need to look up the options of a certain command, you can display its manual using the man command. To look up all options of the ls command, for example, run the following command:

```
pi@raspberrypi ~ $ man ls
```

To scroll down a line, press the down cursor key. Press the up cursor key to scroll up a line. To scroll down a page, press the spacebar. Press Ctrl+B to scroll up a page. To leave the program, press Q.

The man command has many more options. To learn more about it, run the following:

```
pi@raspberrypi ~ $ man man
```

Index

Sound and Arduino!

Add live sound to your apps, and explore the Arduino.

Programming Sound with Pure Data

Sound gives your native, web, or mobile apps that extra dimension, and it's essential for games. Rather than using canned samples from a sample library, learn how to build sounds from the ground up and produce them for web projects using the Pure Data programming language. Even better, you'll be able to integrate dynamic sound environments into your native apps or games—sound that reacts to the app, instead of sounding the same every time. Start your journey as a sound designer, and get the power to craft the sound you put into your digital experiences.

Tony Hillerson
(196 pages) ISBN: 9781937785666. $36
http://pragprog.com/book/thsound

Arduino

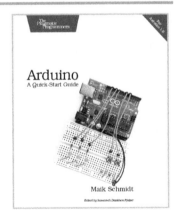

Arduino is an open-source platform that makes DIY electronics projects easier than ever. Even if you have no electronics experience, you'll be creating your first gadgets within a few minutes. Step-by-step instructions show you how to build a universal remote, a motion-sensing game controller, and many other fun, useful projects. This book has now been updated for Arduino 1.0, with revised code, examples, and screenshots throughout. We've changed all the book's examples and added new examples showing how to use the Arduino IDE's new features.

Maik Schmidt
(272 pages) ISBN: 9781934356661. $35
http://pragprog.com/book/msard

Long Live the Command Line!

Use tmux and Vim for incredible mouse-free productivity.

tmux

Your mouse is slowing you down. The time you spend context switching between your editor and your consoles eats away at your productivity. Take control of your environment with tmux, a terminal multiplexer that you can tailor to your workflow. Learn how to customize, script, and leverage tmux's unique abilities and keep your fingers on your keyboard's home row.

Brian P. Hogan
(88 pages) ISBN: 9781934356968. $16.25
http://pragprog.com/book/bhtmux

Practical Vim

Vim is a fast and efficient text editor that will make you a faster and more efficient developer. It's available on almost every OS—if you master the techniques in this book, you'll never need another text editor. In more than 100 Vim tips, you'll quickly learn the editor's core functionality and tackle your trickiest editing and writing tasks.

Drew Neil
(346 pages) ISBN: 9781934356982. $29
http://pragprog.com/book/dnvim

Android and Processing

Script your Android device right on the device, and explore Processing on Android for faster development.

Developing Android on Android

Take advantage of the open, tinker-friendly Android platform and make your device work the way you want it to. Quickly create Android tasks, scripts, and programs entirely on your Android device—no PC required. Learn how to build your own innovative Android programs and workflows with tools you can run on Android itself, and tailor the Android default user interface to match your mobile lifestyle needs. Apply your favorite scripting language to rapidly develop programs that speak the time and battery level, alert you to important events or locations, read your new email to you, and much more.

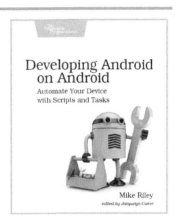

Mike Riley
(232 pages) ISBN: 9781937785543. $36
http://pragprog.com/book/mrand

3D Game Programming for Kids

You know what's even better than playing games? Creating your own. Even if you're an absolute beginner, this book will teach you how to make your own online games with interactive examples. You'll learn programming using nothing more than a browser, and see cool, 3D results as you type. You'll learn real-world programming skills in a real programming language: Java-Script, the language of the web. You'll be amazed at what you can do as you build interactive worlds and fun games. Appropriate for ages 10-99!

Chris Strom
(250 pages) ISBN: 9781937785444. $36
http://pragprog.com/book/csjava

Seven in Seven

From Web Frameworks to Concurrency Models, see what the rest of the world is doing with this introduction to seven different approaches.

Seven Web Frameworks in Seven Weeks

Whether you need a new tool or just inspiration, *Seven Web Frameworks in Seven Weeks* explores modern options, giving you a taste of each with ideas that will help you create better apps. You'll see frameworks that leverage modern programming languages, employ unique architectures, live client-side instead of server-side, or embrace type systems. You'll see everything from familiar Ruby and JavaScript to the more exotic Erlang, Haskell, and Clojure.

Jack Moffitt, Fred Daoud
(302 pages) ISBN: 9781937785635. $38
http://pragprog.com/book/7web

Seven Concurrency Models in Seven Weeks

Your software needs to leverage multiple cores, handle thousands of users and terabytes of data, and continue working in the face of both hardware and software failure. Concurrency and parallelism are the keys, and *Seven Concurrency Models in Seven Weeks* equips you for this new world. See how emerging technologies such as actors and functional programming address issues with traditional threads and locks development. Learn how to exploit the parallelism in your computer's GPU and leverage clusters of machines with Map-Reduce and Stream Processing. And do it all with the confidence that comes from using tools that help you write crystal clear, high-quality code.

Paul Butcher
(300 pages) ISBN: 9781937785659. $38
http://pragprog.com/book/pb7con

Put the "Fun" in Functional

Elixir puts the "fun" back into functional programming, on top of the robust, battle-tested, industrial-strength environment of Erlang.

Programming Elixir

You want to explore functional programming, but are put off by the academic feel (tell me about monads just one more time). You know you need concurrent applications, but also know these are almost impossible to get right. Meet Elixir, a functional, concurrent language built on the rock-solid Erlang VM. Elixir's pragmatic syntax and built-in support for metaprogramming will make you productive and keep you interested for the long haul. This book is *the* introduction to Elixir for experienced programmers.

Dave Thomas
(240 pages) ISBN: 9781937785581. $36
http://pragprog.com/book/elixir

Programming Erlang (2nd edition)

A multi-user game, web site, cloud application, or networked database can have thousands of users all interacting at the same time. You need a powerful, industrial-strength tool to handle the really hard problems inherent in parallel, concurrent environments. You need Erlang. In this second edition of the best-selling *Programming Erlang*, you'll learn how to write parallel programs that scale effortlessly on multicore systems.

Joe Armstrong
(548 pages) ISBN: 9781937785536. $42
http://pragprog.com/book/jaerlang2

The Pragmatic Bookshelf

The Pragmatic Bookshelf features books written by developers for developers. The titles continue the well-known Pragmatic Programmer style and continue to garner awards and rave reviews. As development gets more and more difficult, the Pragmatic Programmers will be there with more titles and products to help you stay on top of your game.

Visit Us Online

This Book's Home Page
http://pragprog.com/book/msraspi2
Source code from this book, errata, and other resources. Come give us feedback, too!

Register for Updates
http://pragprog.com/updates
Be notified when updates and new books become available.

Join the Community
http://pragprog.com/community
Read our weblogs, join our online discussions, participate in our mailing list, interact with our wiki, and benefit from the experience of other Pragmatic Programmers.

New and Noteworthy
http://pragprog.com/news
Check out the latest pragmatic developments, new titles and other offerings.

Contact Us

Online Orders:	*http://pragprog.com/catalog*
Customer Service:	*support@pragprog.com*
International Rights:	*translations@pragprog.com*
Academic Use:	*academic@pragprog.com*
Write for Us:	*http://pragprog.com/write-for-us*
Or Call:	+1 800-699-7764

CPSIA information can be obtained at www.ICGtesting.com
Printed in the USA
LVOW02s1651110514

385310LV00003B/14/P